GW00703502

Companion to
the Sunday Gospels

The Year of Mercy

by
Dom Henry Wansbrough

*All booklets are published thanks to the
generous support of the members of the
Catholic Truth Society*

CATHOLIC TRUTH SOCIETY
PUBLISHERS TO THE HOLY SEE

The Jerusalem Bible translation

The Jerusalem Bible was first published in 1966. It was produced by a team of distinguished English scholars (including J.R.R. Tolkien), working under Alexander Jones. It made available for English readers the findings of the French Bible de Jérusalem published a decade earlier by the famous French biblical school in Jerusalem, the first Catholic Bible edition to incorporate all the advances of modern biblical study. The Jerusalem Bible was the first translation of the whole Bible into modern English, and as such has maintained its status as authorised for use in the liturgy.

Acknowledgements

CTS gratefully acknowledges the publishers of *The Sunday Word* for their permission to reproduce some of Fr Wansbrough's material in this publication.

Images: Page 34: *The Return of the Prodigal Son* (oil on canvas) c. 1630's, Italian School, (17th century) / © Dulwich Picture Gallery, London, UK / Bridgeman Images.

Page 45: *Christ Carrying His Cross*, 1535 (oil on panel), Palmezzano, Marco (1458-1539) / © Leeds Museums and Art Galleries (Temple Newsam House) UK / Bridgeman Images.

ISBN 978 1 78469 103 5

Foreword by Cardinal Vincent Nichols
Archbishop of Westminster

Pope Francis has declared the year from 8th December 2015 till 20th November 2016 a Jubilee of Mercy. So, with great attentiveness to our Holy Father, we are all to think deeply about what is meant by the mercy of God and about how it enters our lives and about all that this mercy asks of us. The mercy of God is the shape taken by God's love in the face of the mess we make of our lives and of our world. The love and mercy of God are inseparable. Both are shown in everything that God gives to us: our very existence, our faith, our vocation or calling in life, the commandments, the sacraments of the Church, the gift of prayer - all are rightly to be understood as the gift of God's mercy. Creation is God's first act of mercy: he has created me when there is no absolute need for me ever to exist; he has created me to know him, love him and serve him and to be happy with him forever. This is God's great mercy: that my life is not pointless, futile, as many secretly fear, but crowned with a most glorious destiny: to be with him for all eternity. The deepest desire of the Father's heart is that I achieve that glorious destiny. And to make that come about, God pours out upon me an endless stream of mercy, never tiring in his love.

In the person of Jesus we see God's mercy fully revealed. In him we not only see our destiny spelt out in full, but also the remarkable way in which God makes it possible for us to attain that destiny. For each one of us Jesus is indeed our beginning and our end, our Alpha and our Omega.

Rome, October 2015

Jesus said to his disciples: 'There will be signs in the sun and moon and stars; on earth nations in agony, bewildered by the clamour of the ocean and its waves; men dying of fear as they await what menaces the world, for the powers of heaven will be shaken. And then they will see the Son of Man coming in a cloud with power and great glory. When these things begin to take place, stand erect, hold your heads high, because your liberation is near at hand.

'Watch yourselves, or your hearts will be coarsened with debauchery and drunkenness and the cares of life, and that day will be sprung on you suddenly, like a trap. For it will come down on every living man on the face of the earth. Stay awake, praying at all times for the strength to survive all that is going to happen, and to stand with confidence before the Son of Man.'

Liberation is Near at Hand

The first Sunday Gospel of the year (and the liturgical year begins in Advent) is also in a way the last Gospel of the previous year. It comes at the end of Jesus's ministry, when he is preparing his disciples for their own ministry - in succession to him. Jesus is speaking to them on the Mount of Olives, looking down on the white city of Jerusalem, glittering in the sunshine. The city is soon to be destroyed by the Romans, with dreadful horrors of famine, massacre, burnings and executions. This is seen as a foretaste of the end of the world when Jesus, the Son of Man, comes to save his people.

We do not know when this will happen, and, more importantly, when it will happen *for us*, when we will meet the Son of Man and be judged and saved by him. But our Christian faith is a guarantee that it will be a moment of God's mercy, whenever it occurs. We must look forward to it, and have it ever present before our mind. But we would be fooling ourselves if we think that there are no struggles and trials and hardships to be undergone on the way.

Why is the passage appointed for the first Sunday of Advent, the turning-point between the years? Because the birth of Jesus at Christmas, for which we are beginning to prepare, is a significant move towards the fulfilment of the promises of salvation, the coming of Christ as a baby - with all the budding potential of a baby.

In the fifteenth year of Tiberius Caesar's reign, when Pontius Pilate was governor of Judaea, Herod tetrarch of Galilee, his brother Philip tetrarch of the lands of Ituraea and Trachonitis, Lysanias tetrarch of Abilene, during the pontificate of Annas and Caiaphas, the word of God came to John son of Zechariah, in the wilderness. He went through the whole Jordan district proclaiming a baptism of repentance for the forgiveness of sins, as it is written in the book of sayings of the prophet Isaiah:

A voice cries in the wilderness:
Prepare a way for the Lord,
make his paths straight.
Every valley will be filled in,
every mountain and hill be laid low,
winding ways will be straightened
and rough roads made smooth.
And all mankind shall see the salvation of God.

SECOND SUNDAY OF ADVENT

The Baptist's Message

This Gospel reading is like a drum-roll at the beginning of a show, building up the excitement. First comes a drum-roll of human history, the names of the great rulers of the world. Then comes a drum-roll of God's history, the promise of Isaiah that all the crooked places of the world are to be straightened out.

John the Baptist, a daunting prophetic figure, came out of the desert and stood at the Jordan, catching all the merchants and travellers as they forded the river on the main trading route to the East, intent on their commercial and secular aims. 'No!' he cries, 'you have got to change your standards, take on a different set of values, for something much more important is about to happen.' This is what 'Repent!' means: 'Change your way of life! Get real! Join the community of those who are waiting for the Great Event! The moment of God's mercy is approaching. This is going to change everything and bring in a totally new world.'

If we take John's message seriously we must examine ourselves and our priorities in life. What is important to us? Are we building a community where God's true values are our guiding-lines? Are we making his paths straight and the rough roads smooth?

When all the people asked John, 'What must we do?' he answered, 'If anyone has two tunics he must share with the man who has none, and the one with something to eat must do the same.' There were tax collectors too who came for baptism, and these said to him, 'Master what must we do?' He said to them, 'Exact no more than your rate.' Some soldiers asked him in their turn, 'What about us? What must we do?' He said to them, 'No intimidation! No extortion! Be content with your pay!'

A feeling of expectancy had grown among the people, who were beginning to think that John might be the Christ, so John declared before them all, 'I baptise you with water, but someone is coming, someone who is more powerful than I am, and I am not fit to undo the strap of his sandals; he will baptise you with the Holy Spirit and fire. His winnowing-fan is in his hand to clear his threshing-floor and to gather the wheat into his barn; but the chaff he will burn in a fire that will never go out.' As well as this, there were many other things he said to exhort the people and to announce the Good News to them.

John the Baptist's Counsels

The third Sunday of Advent in each cycle always shows John the Baptist pointing out Jesus, and so increasing the excitement of the coming Messiah. But we must prepare for the Messiah, and first John teaches various groups of people what they must do to prepare; they are willing but need guidance. Basically John's instruction is not to exploit the weak; if they want to be baptised into the community of the Messiah they must not take advantage of the poor. This is an early example of a beautiful attitude we shall see all through the Gospel of Luke: he is always sensitive to the needs of the weak, and especially the possibilities of the powerful victimising the poor. He is very aware of the dangers of money, so he stresses the danger of tax-collectors squirrelling away funds into their own pockets and of soldiers grousing about their pay. In the modern world, too, money often challenges our relationships: when money is mentioned everything can turn sour.

In the second half of this reading it is interesting to see how the Baptist's idea of the Messiah differs from Jesus's own idea. Both see the coming of the Messiah as the time of decision and separation. But, while John sees it as the time of destruction of sinners (the chaff burnt in the fire), Jesus sees it as a time when the mercy of God goes out to sinners and brings them into the fold.

Mary set out and went as quickly as she could to a town in the hill country of Judah. She went into Zechariah's house and greeted Elizabeth. Now as soon as Elizabeth heard Mary's greeting, the child leapt in her womb and Elizabeth was filled with the Holy Spirit. She gave a loud cry and said, 'Of all women you are the most blessed, and blessed is the fruit of your womb. Why should I be honoured with a visit from the mother of my Lord? For the moment your greeting reached my ears, the child in my womb leapt for joy. Yes, blessed is she who believed that the promise made her by the Lord would be fulfilled.'

The Visitation

Luke's Gospel is perhaps the book of the Bible which is most sensitive to women. Zechariah heard the message of the angel and had difficulty in believing it; Mary heard the message of the angel and believed it in humble puzzlement. As we prepare for the birth of Jesus, Luke gives us a picture of the two mothers-to-be exchanging greetings and touchingly sharing their joy in motherhood. The enthusiasm and generosity of the young girl in making the arduous week-long journey from Nazareth is answered by the gratitude of the elderly woman and by the excitement of the unborn baby.

The stories of the births of the two boys are intertwined to show the similarities and differences between them. John is to be the last and the greatest of Old Testament prophets; Jesus is to be the fulfilment of all the hopes of the Old Testament. Zechariah's song of joy at his son's birth points to his role in preparing the way; Mary's song of joy at her Son's birth dwells on the fulfilment and the outpouring of God's mercy from generation to generation of the future.

How much did the two mothers know of the rejection to be suffered by each of the sons? Did they remember that the Servant of the Lord in the Old Testament had to suffer? Mary was mysteriously warned by Simeon when she brought Jesus into the Temple, but - like ourselves - she had to wait to see what the Lord had in store for her.

Every year the parents of Jesus used to go to Jerusalem for the feast of the Passover. When he was twelve years old, they went up for the feast as usual. When they were on their way home after the feast, the boy Jesus stayed behind in Jerusalem without his parents knowing it. They assumed he was with the caravan, and it was only after a day's journey that they went to look for him among their relations and acquaintances. When they failed to find him they went back to Jerusalem looking for him everywhere.

Three days later, they found him in the Temple, sitting among the doctors, listening to them, and asking them questions; and all those who heard him were astounded at his intelligence and his replies. They were overcome when they saw him, and his mother said to him, 'My child, why have you done this to us? See how worried your father and I have been, looking for you.' 'Why were you looking for me?' he replied. 'Did you not know that I must be busy with my Father's affairs?' But they did not understand what he meant.

He then went down with them and came to Nazareth and lived under their authority. His mother stored up all these things in her heart. And Jesus increased in wisdom, in stature, and in favour with God and men.

The Child Jesus in the Temple

This is the only story in all the Gospels of the child Jesus acting on his own. It raises the fascinating question: what was he like as a child - a divine child, yes, but growing, learning, developing as a human child. There can have been no evil in him, but human children learn only by getting things wrong: he must have made mistakes and learned from them. What was the wonderful relationship between him and Joseph and Mary, who taught him the loving mercy of God? He must have recognised it in himself as he grew and - like any child - came to know himself. He does not harangue the teachers of the Law, he only sits easily among them and puts to them questions - those devastatingly simple questions of a child. Yet in his answers they are astounded to recognise the deepest Wisdom from which these questions spring.

Like any twelve-year-old, he wanders off on his own business, quite oblivious of the worry it gives his parents. When they eventually track him down, he obliviously says, 'Oh, didn't you know...?' Mary, the perfect mother, does not explode ('You might have told us!') but recognises the twelve-year-old. She knows his deepest longing, his need to be with the Father about whom they have taught him.

After Jesus had been born at Bethlehem in Judaea during the reign of King Herod, some wise men came to Jerusalem from the east. 'Where is the infant king of the Jews?' they asked. 'We saw his star as it rose and have come to do him homage.' When King Herod heard this he was perturbed, and so was the whole of Jerusalem. He called together all the chief priests and the scribes of the people, and enquired of them where the Christ was to be born. 'At Bethlehem in Judaea,' they told him 'for this is what the prophet wrote:

> And you, Bethlehem, in the land of Judah
> you are by no means least among the leaders of Judah,
> for out of you will come a leader
> who will shepherd my people Israel.'

Then Herod summoned the wise men to see him privately. He asked them the exact date on which the star had appeared, and sent them on to Bethlehem. 'Go and find out all about the child,' he said 'and when you have found him, let me know, so that I too may go and do him homage.' Having listened to what the king had to say, they set out. And there in front of them was the star they had seen rising; it went forward and halted over the place where the child was. The sight of the star filled them with delight, and going into the house they saw the child with his mother Mary, and falling to their knees they did him homage. Then, opening their treasures, they offered him gifts of gold and frankincense and myrrh. But they were warned in a dream not to go back to Herod, and returned to their own country by a different way.

FEAST OF THE EPIPHANY

Wise Men from the East

In the eastern Church the feast of the Epiphany, rather than the actual day of birth, is considered the real celebration of the coming of Christ as man. 'Epiphany' means 'public appearance' or 'manifestation' and the feast celebrates the appearance of Christ to all the world - or to the whole universe, for the coming of Wise Men from the East (the East is the home of Wisdom - remember the Wizard of Oz) is equivalent to visitors from outer space. They lay their fabulous gifts, the wealth and perfumes of the East, at the feet of the new-born King in homage. This is the fulfilment of the promises of Isaiah, camels in throngs coming from Sheba bringing gold and incense and singing the praise of the Lord.

Indeed the star also symbolises the homage of the whole universe. It would be a mistake to search the records for a suitable star, for at that time the appearance of a star in the heavens was a way of saying that a 'star' had been born on earth. A star appeared at the birth of Nimrod, of Julius Caesar and of others. But no one else had the star moving in the heavens and as though bending in homage over the birthplace itself.

A feeling of expectancy had grown among the people, who were beginning to think that John might be the Christ, so John declared before them all, 'I baptise you with water, but someone is coming, someone who is more powerful than I am and I am not fit to undo the strap of his sandals; he will baptise you with the Holy Spirit and fire.'

Now when all the people had been baptised and while Jesus after his own baptism was at prayer, heaven opened and the Holy Spirit descended on him in bodily shape, like a dove. And a voice came from heaven, 'You are my Son, the Beloved; my favour rests on you.'

The Coming of the Spirit

In contrast to the account in Mark and Matthew, the story as told by Luke is not so much the Baptism of Jesus as the Coming of the Spirit on Jesus just after his baptism, 'when he was at prayer'. John the Baptist has announced the coming of one more powerful than himself, and by his baptising has prepared a community. But then he disappears, carried off by Herod; he is not mentioned as being there to baptise Jesus himself. After this, throughout the Gospel of Luke, the Spirit leads Jesus: he makes his first dramatic proclamation at Nazareth, 'filled with the Spirit', announcing that the Spirit of the Lord is upon him, a Spirit which will reach out to the whole world. In the same way, the mission of the apostles begins at Pentecost with the coming of the Spirit upon them in the Upper Room, and the Spirit of Jesus guides them at every stage of the Acts of the Apostles.

The early Church was full of the consciousness of the presence of the Spirit among them. Paul writes so frequently of the transforming power of the Spirit in the community, making it the Body of Christ, in which every member has a special part to play. Are we more sluggish and less responsive than they were in the early days? Perhaps we should rejoice more in the presence of Christ's Spirit among us.

There was a wedding at Cana in Galilee. The mother of Jesus was there, and Jesus and his disciples had also been invited. When they ran out of wine, since the wine provided for the wedding was all finished, the mother of Jesus said to him, 'They have no wine.' Jesus said, 'Woman why turn to me? My hour has not come yet.' His mother said to the servants, 'Do whatever he tells you.' There were six stone water jars standing there, meant for the ablutions that are customary among the Jews; each could hold twenty or thirty gallons. Jesus said to the servants, 'Fill the jars with water,' and they filled them to the brim. 'Draw some out now' he told them 'and take it to the steward.' They did this; the steward tasted the water, and it had turned into wine. Having no idea where it came from - only the servants who had drawn the water knew - the steward called the bridegroom and said, 'People generally serve the best wine first, and keep the cheaper sort till the guests have plenty to drink; but you have kept the best wine till now.'

This was the first of the signs given by Jesus: it was given at Cana in Galilee. He let his glory be seen, and his disciples believed in him.

The Wedding-feast at Cana

What makes the marriage-feast at Cana so special, that it should be the first of the Gospels of the Ordinary Sundays of the Year, and allow the intrusion of the Gospel of John into the Year of Luke? One special point is Jesus' enjoyment and encouragement of festivities. He was no kill-joy, but enjoyed celebrating with others; his opponents accused him of being a glutton and a drunkard. It was at this party that the disciples first came to believe in him and saw his glory! And the point of this wedding-feast is that it is a foretaste of the final wedding-feast of heaven.

Another point, not so comfortable, is that this gives us the first mention of the Hour of Jesus. This 'Hour' will stalk us right through the Gospel of John. What is it? Twice his opponents try to arrest him, but his Hour has not yet come. It will come to its moment in the Passion and Resurrection of the Lord, the glorious triumph won through hideous suffering, and right from the start Jesus knows that he is destined for this. Why at the start of this series of readings from Luke? Perhaps it is the way Mary's request seems to bend Jesus's stern put-down, 'My Hour has not yet come'. Luke is always writing about the power and importance of prayer, and here his mother's prayer wins her request. That is the way to gain the Lord's mercy!

Seeing that many others have undertaken to draw up accounts of the events that have taken place among us, exactly as these were handed down to us by those who from the outset were eyewitnesses and ministers of the word, I in my turn, after carefully going over the whole story from the beginning, have decided to write an ordered account for you, Theophilus, so that your Excellency may learn how well founded the teaching is that you have received.

Jesus, with the power of the Spirit in him, returned to Galilee; and his reputation spread throughout the countryside. He taught in their synagogues and everyone praised him.

He came to Nazara, where he had been brought up, and went into the synagogue on the sabbath day as he usually did. He stood up to read, and they handed him the scroll of the prophet Isaiah. Unrolling the scroll he found the place where it is written:

> The spirit of the Lord has been given to me, for he has
> anointed me.
> He has sent me to bring the good news to the poor,
> to proclaim liberty to captives
> and to the blind new sight,
> to set the downtrodden free,
> to proclaim the Lord's year of favour.

He then rolled up the scroll, gave it back to the assistant and sat down. And all eyes in the synagogue were fixed on him. Then he began to speak to them, 'This text is being fulfilled today even as you listen.'

Jesus Proclaims his Message

This Gospel reading is the first of the straight series of readings from Luke's account of the Good News of Jesus. So it falls into two halves, both of them concerned with beginnings. The first half of the reading is the beginning of the Gospel of Luke, explaining his purpose and methods: Luke's Gospel is founded on good evidence, but is a carefully 'ordered account' to convey Luke's own view, an inspired view of the meaning and message of Jesus.

Then we jump to another beginning, Jesus's first, programmatic proclamation in the synagogue of Nazareth, his home town. Filled with the Spirit - one might almost say 'bubbling with the Spirit' - he proclaims that he has come to fulfil the promises to Israel. Yet it is not Israel who will receive him, although it is the fulfilment of the prophecies of Isaiah. His own town will reject him and he will bring his message of salvation far beyond Israel, to the poor, to captives, to the blind and the downtrodden. It is a proclamation of God's mercy to all who need it most. The first pre-requisite of receiving God's mercy in Jesus is to recognise that we are in that state of need. The disciples, from Peter downwards, must first admit that they are sinners before they accept the call to join the company of Jesus.

Jesus began to speak in the synagogue, 'This text is being fulfilled today even as you listen.' And he won the approval of all, and they were astonished by the gracious words that came from his lips.

They said, 'This is Joseph's son, surely?' But he replied, 'No doubt you will quote me the saying, "Physician, heal yourself" and tell me, "We have heard all that happened in Capernaum, do the same here in your own countryside."' And he went on, 'I tell you solemnly, no prophet is ever accepted in his own country.

'There were many widows in Israel, I can assure you, in Elijah's day, when heaven remained shut for three years and six months and a great famine raged throughout the land, but Elijah was not sent to any one of these: he was sent to a widow at Zarephath, a Sidonian town. And in the prophet Elisha's time there were many lepers in Israel, but none of these was cured, except the Syrian, Naaman.'

Jesus is Rejected at Nazareth

This Sunday's Gospel continues last Sunday's excerpt: Jesus is still making his initial proclamation in the synagogue of Nazareth. He now goes on to say that the Chosen People of Israel are not the only recipients of God's mercy, and there have been occasions when mercy has been granted to others in preference to the Chosen People. This infuriated the hearers to the extent that they wanted to throw him off the cliff.

It is a real problem for us, too, when we see radiant sanctity outside the Catholic Church or even outside the Christian Churches, especially when at the same time we see so much unacceptable behaviour within our own Church. We can accept that God wills all people to be saved, as it says in 1 Timothy. We know that Holy Mother Church is designated as holy, but not all her members follow Christ closely, and we ourselves do not always succeed in following Christ. Since Vatican II we can and must accept that God's call comes in many different ways, even to those whose belief in God and whose commitment to God's values are expressed in very different terms and images. God's mercy comes in many different forms, and it is humbling to realise that we ourselves sometimes put more obstacles in its way (like sunblock against the sun's rays) than many non-Christians, non-Catholics.

Jesus was standing one day by the lake of Gennesaret, with the crowd pressing round him listening to the word of God, when he caught sight of two boats close to the bank. The fishermen had gone out of them and were washing their nets. He got into one of the boats - it was Simon's - and asked him to put out a little from the shore. Then he sat down and taught the crowds from the boat.

When he had finished speaking he said to Simon, 'Put out into deep water and pay out your nets for a catch.' 'Master,' Simon replied 'we worked hard all night long and caught nothing, but if you say so, I will pay out the nets.' And when they had done this they netted such a huge number of fish that their nets began to tear, so they signalled to their companions in the other boats to come and help them; when these came, they filled the two boats to sinking point.

When Simon Peter saw this he fell at the knees of Jesus saying 'Leave me, Lord; I am a sinful man.' For he and all his companions were completely overcome by the catch they had made; so also were James and John, sons of Zebedee, who were Simon's partners. But Jesus said to Simon, 'Do not be afraid; from now on it is men you will catch.' Then, bringing their boats back to land, they left everything and followed him.

The Call of the First Disciples

There are two stories of an amazing catch of fish after a night of total failure, each of them leading to Peter receiving a commission in the company of Christ's disciples. One comes here, early in the ministry; the other comes in John 21, the third time Jesus showed himself to his disciples after the Resurrection. Are they the same incident, or were there two similar incidents? A further question, was Peter called to be with Jesus now for the first time, or was he called by Jesus, totally unknown, walking along the lakeside, as Mark (1:16-18) and Matthew represent it?

In both stories we are reminded of Peter's failure and sin before Jesus gives him the charge. In today's version Peter responds to Jesus's call by blurting out, 'Leave me, Lord, I am a sinner'. In the version of John, Peter is reminded of his failure by being made to express three times his love of Jesus. Each of these details has the same comforting message: Jesus does not demand perfect material in those whom he calls to be his company: we do not need to be perfect before being called; he enjoys the company of sinners. Even more: Jesus can tolerate failure even after the call, provided that we acknowledge our failures and whole-heartedly attest our love for Jesus. In Jesus's eyes there is no such thing as a hopeless failure.

Filled with the Holy Spirit, Jesus left the Jordan and was led by the Spirit through the wilderness being tempted there by the devil for forty days. During that time he ate nothing and at the end he was hungry. Then the devil said to him, 'If you are the Son of God, tell this stone to turn into a loaf.' But Jesus replied 'Scripture says: Man does not live on bread alone.'

Then leading him to a height, the devil showed him in a moment of time all the kingdoms of the world and said to him, 'I will give you all this power and the glory of these kingdoms, for it has been committed to me and I give it to anyone I choose. Worship me, then, and it shall all be yours.' But Jesus answered him, 'Scripture says:

You must worship the Lord your God,
and serve him alone.'

Then he led him to Jerusalem and made him stand on the parapet of the Temple. 'If you are the Son of God,' he said to him 'throw yourself down from here, for scripture says:

He will put his angels in charge of you to guard you,
and again:

They will hold you up on their hands
in case you hurt your foot against a stone.'

But Jesus answered him, 'It has been said:

You must not put the Lord your God to the test.'

Having exhausted all these ways of tempting him, the devil left him, to return at the appointed time.

Jesus is Tested in the Desert

For Luke the baptism of Jesus is the moment when he is filled with the Spirit; the voice from heaven declares to us that he is God's beloved Son. And so Jesus goes out into the desert, filled with the Spirit. This is surely a withdrawal to prepare in the company of his Father for his mission as God's Chosen One. As God's Son he is to show God's face to the world. How should he show it? The biblical dialogue with Satan, as they throw texts at each other, must represent the false ways of showing God's face, suggested to Jesus and rejected by him. Each has its attractions!

The first, turning stones into food (after forty days without food) is the temptation to bring merely material prosperity; this is ultimately unsatisfying, and not the way of God. The second is the worship of power, domination of the whole world. That is not the way of Jesus, who invites us to follow him as willing companions in the supreme liberty of love. But what is the third temptation? Is it to test God by showy miracles, casting himself down from the height of the Temple? Or is it a temptation to leave it all to God, to test God by sitting back and letting God's unseen messengers, the angels, do the hard work? No, Jesus is given the Spirit to do God's work - and so are we all, as members of his Body.

Jesus took with him Peter and John and James and went up the mountain to pray. As he prayed, the aspect of his face was changed and his clothing became brilliant as lightning. Suddenly there were two men there talking to him; they were Moses and Elijah appearing in glory, and they were speaking of his passing which he was to accomplish in Jerusalem. Peter and his companions were heavy with sleep, but they kept awake and saw his glory and the two men standing with him. As these were leaving him, Peter said to Jesus, 'Master, it is wonderful for us to be here; so let us make three tents, one for you, one for Moses and one for Elijah.' - He did not know what he was saying. As he spoke, a cloud came and covered them with shadow; and when they went into the cloud the disciples were afraid. And a voice came from the cloud saying, 'This is my Son, the Chosen One. Listen to him.' And after the voice had spoken, Jesus was found alone. The disciples kept silence and, at that time, told no one what they had seen.

The Transfiguration

The Transfiguration provides the disciples with a glimpse of Christ's divine glory on the holy mountain. He is seen as a heavenly figure, transformed and with his clothing dazzling white. His full status is hinted also by the presence of Moses and Elijah, who both experienced the presence of the LORD on the holy mountain. Which holy mountain? We do not know where the Transfiguration happened: the location is unimportant, the daunting holiness is everything. On Sinai Moses begged to see the LORD and was given a vision of the divine glory from the shelter of a cleft in the rock. On Mount Horeb Elijah experienced the LORD not in wind, fire or earthquake but in the awesome 'sound of silence'. So at the Transfiguration Jesus himself is seen as the LORD, soon to be wrapped in the cloud of divinity. Peter shows the reaction to the divinity: stunned with fear and awe, he still treasures the moment and yearns to prolong it for ever, to dwell in the presence of the LORD.

Luke's account has two special treasures. Jesus is at prayer when he is transfigured. Luke often shows that every important event in Jesus's life begins with prayer: the baptism and descent of the Spirit, the choice of the Twelve, the teaching of the Lord's Prayer, the arrest in the Garden of Olives. Also, the three are speaking about his 'exodus' at Jerusalem: he is about to begin his journey up to Jerusalem, where he will suffer and be glorified.

Some people arrived and told Jesus about the Galileans whose blood Pilate had mingled with that of their sacrifices. At this he said to them, 'Do you suppose these Galileans who suffered like that were greater sinners than any other Galileans? They were not, I tell you. No; but unless you repent you will all perish as they did. Or those eighteen on whom the tower at Siloam fell and killed them? Do you suppose that they were more guilty than all the other people living in Jerusalem? They were not, I tell you. No; but unless you repent you will all perish as they did.'

He told this parable: 'A man had a fig tree planted in his vineyard, and he came looking for fruit on it but found none. He said to the man who looked after the vineyard, "Look here, for three years now I have been coming to look for fruit on this fig tree and finding none. Cut it down: why should it be taking up the ground?" "Sir," the man replied "leave it one more year and give me time to dig round it and manure it: it may bear fruit next year; if not, then you can cut it down."'

Time for Repentance

Throughout his writings, the Gospel and the Acts of the
Apostles, Luke concentrates on the need to repent. John
the Baptist proclaims repentance; in the Acts Stephen, Peter
and Paul all end their speeches with an appeal to repent.
This does not mean getting all dewy-eyed and self-pitying
about our sins and wickedness; it means changing our way
of life, accepting God's ways, God's will and values and
standards as our own. The Greek word means 'change your
mind' or 'a change of heart'. The Hebrew word behind it
means 'turn round and go in the opposite direction'. It is a
radical change of direction.

The two examples of indiscriminate massacre by Pilate
and of indiscriminate accidental death from the tower at
Siloam (perhaps a sort of Ibrox Park disaster) show the
danger of leaving repentance too late. On the other side
of the coin, the parable of the fig-tree gives hope. Mark
and Matthew use the barren fig-tree at the Cleansing of
the Temple as a symbol of the lethal stubbornness of
the Temple authorities. Luke, the evangelist of hope and
repentance, takes the threat and turns it into a parable
of hope. God offers the fig-tree every possible chance to
respond to the loving care of his servant.

As we prepare to join Jesus in his cross and Resurrection
at Easter, this is a good time to consider the standards by
which we really conduct our lives.

FOURTH SUNDAY OF LENT

The Prodigal Son

LUKE 15:1-3,11-32

The tax collectors and the sinners were all seeking the company of Jesus to hear what he had to say, and the Pharisees and the scribes complained. 'This man' they said 'welcomes sinners and eats with them.' So he spoke this parable to them:

'A man had two sons. The younger said to his father, "Father, let me have the share of the estate that would come to me." So the father divided the property between them. A few days later, the younger son got together everything he had and left for a distant country where he squandered his money on a life of debauchery.

'When he had spent it all, that country experienced a severe famine, and now he began to feel the pinch, so he hired himself out to one of the local inhabitants who put him on his farm to feed the pigs. And he would willingly have filled his belly with the husks the pigs were eating but no one offered him anything. Then he came to his senses and said, "How many of my father's paid servants have more food than they want, and here am I dying of hunger! I will leave this place and go to my father and say: Father, I have sinned against heaven and against you; I no longer deserve to be called your son; treat me as one of your paid servants." So he left the place and went back to his father.

'While he was still a long way off, his father saw him and was moved with pity. He ran to the boy, clasped him in his arms and kissed him tenderly. Then his son said, "Father,

I have sinned against heaven and against you. I no longer deserve to be called your son." But the father said to his servants, "Quick! Bring out the best robe and put it on him; put a ring on his finger and sandals on his feet. Bring the calf we have been fattening, and kill it; we are going to have a feast, a celebration, because this son of mine was dead and has come back to life; he was lost and is found." And they began to celebrate.

'Now the elder son was out in the fields, and on his way back, as he drew near the house, he could hear music and dancing. Calling one of the servants he asked what it was all about. "Your brother has come" replied the servant "and your father has killed the calf we had fattened because he has got him back safe and sound." He was angry then and refused to go in, and his father came out to plead with him; but he answered his father, "Look, all these years I have slaved for you and never once disobeyed your orders, yet you never offered me so much as a kid for me to celebrate with my friends. But, for this son of yours, when he comes back after swallowing up your property - he and his women - you kill the calf we had been fattening."

'The father said, "My son, you are with me always and all I have is yours. But it is only right we should celebrate and rejoice, because your brother here was dead and has come to life; he was lost and is found."'

The Prodigal Son

Who deserves the more sympathy? The younger son is a rascal, no worse. He insults his father by saying he wants the money, whether the father is alive or dead. He is not even really repentant; he just gets hungry and thinks up a way to solve his problem. The dutiful elder son turns out possibly worse: he insults his father by refusing to come into the dinner, even though dad has left his guests at table to persuade him in. He insults his brother ('your son', he calls him) by inventing tales of loose women. But he has worked obediently and patiently for years! The father is the most tragic hero, insulted by both children but never giving up on them. He even trusts the wastrel by giving him power to sign away the rest of his inheritance with his ring. He even neglects his own guests - and a fatted calf would feed the whole village.

Here, then, is the supreme tale of the Father's inalienable mercy; nothing can knock God off track! Here above all we have an illustration of the explanation of the divine Name given to Moses on Sinai, 'a God of tenderness and compassion, slow to anger, rich in kindness and faithfulness' (*Ex* 34). This is the third of three consecutive parables of God's mercy illustrating the joy in heaven equal to the joy on earth of the man who finds his missing hundredth sheep and the woman who finds her lost tenth silver coin.

Jesus went to the Mount of Olives. At daybreak he appeared in the Temple again; and as all the people came to him, he sat down and began to teach them.

The scribes and Pharisees brought a woman along who had been caught committing adultery; and making her stand there in full view of everybody, they said to Jesus, 'Master, this woman was caught in the very act of committing adultery, and Moses has ordered us in the Law to condemn women like this to death by stoning. What have you to say?' They asked him this as a test, looking for something to use against him. But Jesus bent down and started writing on the ground with his finger. As they persisted with their question, he looked up and said, 'If there is one of you who has not sinned, let him be the first to throw a stone at her.' Then he bent down and wrote on the ground again. When they heard this they went away one by one, beginning with the eldest, until Jesus was left alone with the woman, who remained standing there. He looked up and said, 'Woman, where are they? Has no one condemned you?' 'No one, sir,' she replied. 'Neither do I condemn you,' said Jesus 'go away, and don't sin any more.'

The Woman Taken in Adultery

This lovely story of divine forgiveness is absent from some early manuscripts of the Gospel of John, and in different places in others. It may be a very ancient independent story which was eventually fitted in here to illustrate Jesus's saying, 'The Law does not allow us to pass judgement without giving a hearing' (*Jn* 7:51). The most attractive feature is the sensitivity and gentleness of Jesus to the woman: he does not harass her or intrude on her shame; in his loving self-restraint he simply gives her space for her conscience to come to her rescue. It is in silence and peace that our consciences may bring us back to our true senses. Jesus does not judge her, but allows her to judge herself. Throughout the Gospel of John people are judging themselves by their reaction to Jesus: the disciples at Cana, Nicodemus, the Samaritan woman, the man born blind and the Jewish authorities. At the same time he gives the accusers the silence and peace to examine their own consciences and retreat from their angry self-righteousness to a true knowledge of themselves. This is a blueprint of divine mercy.

What was Jesus writing on the ground? We do not even know whether he was literate; the word used could equally well mean 'drawing'. Perhaps he was just doodling to give her time. There was no need to scold her, and he sends her away with a positive encouragement.

The Passion According to Luke

LUKE 23:1-49

N The whole assembly then rose, and they brought him before Pilate.

They began their accusation by saying,

C We found this man inciting our people to revolt, opposing payment of the tribute to Caesar, and claiming to be Christ, a king.

N Pilate put to him this question,

O Are you the king of the Jews?

N He replied,

J It is you who say it.

N Pilate then said to the chief priests and the crowd,

O I find no case against this man.

N But they persisted,

C He is inflaming the people with his teaching all over Judaea; it has come all the way from Galilee, where he started, down to here.

N When Pilate heard this, he asked if the man were a Galilean; and finding that he came under Herod's jurisdiction he passed him over to Herod who was also in Jerusalem at that time.

Herod was delighted to see Jesus; he had heard about him and had been wanting for a long time to set eyes on him; moreover, he was hoping to see some miracle worked by him. So he questioned him at some length; but without getting any reply. Meanwhile the chief priests and the scribes were there, violently pressing their accusations. Then Herod, together with his guards, treated him with contempt and made fun of him; he put a rich cloak on him and sent him back to Pilate. And though Herod and Pilate had been enemies before, they were reconciled that same day.

Pilate then summoned the chief priests and the leading men and the people. He said,

O   You brought this man before me as a political agitator. Now I have gone into the matter myself in your presence and found no case against the man in respect of all the charges you bring against him. Nor has Herod either, since he has sent him back to us. As you can see, the man has done nothing that deserves death, so I shall have him flogged and then let him go.

N   But as one man they howled,

C   Away with him! Give us Barabbas!

N   This man had been thrown into prison for causing a riot in the city and for murder.

Pilate was anxious to set Jesus free and addressed them again, but they shouted back,

C   Crucify him! Crucify him!

N   And for the third time he spoke to them,

O   Why? What harm has this man done? I have found no case against him that deserves death, so I shall have him punished and let him go.

N But they kept on shouting at the top of their voices, demanding that he should be crucified, and their shouts were growing louder.

Pilate then gave his verdict: their demand was to be granted. He released the man they asked for, who had been imprisoned for rioting and murder, and handed Jesus over to them to deal with as they pleased.

As they were leading him away they seized on a man, Simon from Cyrene, who was coming in from the country, and made him shoulder the cross and carry it behind Jesus. Large numbers of people followed him, and of women too who mourned and lamented for him. But Jesus turned to them and said,

J Daughters of Jerusalem, do not weep for me; weep rather for yourselves and for your children. For the days will surely come when people will say, 'Happy are those who are barren, the wombs that have never borne, the breasts that have never suckled!' Then they will begin to say to the mountains, 'Fall on us!'; to the hills, 'Cover us!' For if men use the green wood like this, what will happen when it is dry?

N Now with him they were also leading out two other criminals to be executed.

When they reached the place called The Skull, they crucified him there and the criminals also, one on the right, the other on the left. Jesus said,

J Father, forgive them; they do not know what they are doing.

N Then they cast lots to share out his clothing. The people stayed there watching him. As for the leaders, they jeered at him, saying,

C He saved others; let him save himself if he is the Christ of God, the Chosen One.

N The soldiers mocked him too, and when they approached to offer him vinegar they said,

C If you are the king of the Jews, save yourself.

N Above him there was an inscription: 'This is the King of the Jews.'

One of the criminals hanging there abused him, saying,

O Are you not the Christ? Save yourself and us as well.

N But the other spoke up and rebuked him,

O Have you no fear of God at all? You got the same sentence as he did, but in our case we deserved it: we are paying for what we did. But this man has done nothing wrong. Jesus, remember me when you come into your kingdom.

N He replied,

J Indeed, I promise you, today you will be with me in paradise.

N It was now about the sixth hour and, with the sun eclipsed, a darkness came over the whole land until the ninth hour. The veil of the Temple was torn right down the middle; and when Jesus had cried out in a loud voice, he said,

J   Father, into your hands I commit my spirit.

N   With these words he breathed his last.

All kneel and pause a moment.

When the centurion saw what had taken place, he gave praise to God and said,

O   This was a great and good man.

N   And when all the people who had gathered for the spectacle saw what had happened, they went home beating their breasts.

All his friends stood at a distance; so also did the women who had accompanied him from Galilee, and they saw all this happen.

(Longer version Luke 22:14-23:56)

The Passion According to Luke

Each of the Gospel writers has a slightly different account of the Passion and Death of Jesus, for it was their task not so much to record history as to explain how these dreadful events could be the central focus of the Good News of Jesus Christ. Each has a different emphasis, and that of Luke is precisely repentance and forgiveness by the mercy of God.

1. The account of the Last Supper is not so much an account of the final Passover meal as an account of two incidents. First comes the identification of the traitor, not by name, but stressing the enormity of his betrayal: to betray a friend with whom one has shared a meal, and even more the same dish, is an unthinkable act of treachery. In all the synoptic Gospels next comes the account of the institution of the Eucharist: the focus is on the blood of Jesus which seals the new covenant, a personal covenant promised by the prophets, by which each of us is sealed into a new and intimate relationship with the Lord. Blood is the symbol of life, and the new covenant gives new life. Luke adds a third element, in the Hellenistic manner gathering together sayings of the Master which will underpin the continuation of his mission by the disciples in the Church. Already we look towards Peter's failure and his repentance and forgiveness.

2. The Agony in the Garden has a new angle. Luke's accent is not on Jesus falling to the ground in distraught anticipation of the torture to come. Instead, he kneels nobly

in fervent prayer, as an example for his followers, 'Pray that you enter not into temptation'. At the arrest he continues his saving mission by healing the man whose ear has been cut off.

3. At Peter's betrayal in the courtyard of the high priest's house the tender glance of Jesus brings Peter to repentance; he bursts into bitter tears and disappears from the scene. The subsequent interrogation (Luke positions it in the morning, not in the night) is more a disorderly kangaroo court. There is no sign of the high priest, and the rabble merely ask Jesus to identify himself as Christ/Messiah and son of God. This Jesus does, adding his own preferred title of 'Son of Man', no doubt with allusion to the glorious Son of Man in Daniel's vision who 'from now on' will be coming on the clouds of heaven.

4. In the trial before Pilate all the accent is on Pilate's desperate attempts to evade responsibility, even sending Jesus over to Herod Antipas, the ruler of Galilee - with the one result that the friendship between Pilate and Herod is restored. Pilate suggests that Jesus should be whipped rather than brutally flogged, but finally rejects all responsibility by handing him over to the Jews to do with him as they wish.

5. In Luke the mission of Jesus to Jerusalem is bracketed at he enters the city by his weeping over its refusal to repent, and now as he leaves the city by his warning to the mourning women of the horrors of the coming siege and sack of Jerusalem. Then at the Crucifixion itself there follows a scene characterised above all by repentance and forgiveness. Jesus forgives his executioners, then the 'good

thief' admits his guilt and turns to Jesus for forgiveness. Jesus promises him Paradise, and in full control yields his spirit into the hands of the Father. Finally the centurion gives glory to God and the crowds depart, beating their breasts in repentance.

It was very early on the first day of the week and still dark, when Mary of Magdala came to the tomb. She saw that the stone had been moved away from the tomb and came running to Simon Peter and the other disciple, the one Jesus loved. 'They have taken the Lord out of the tomb' she said 'and we don't know where they have put him.'

So Peter set out with the other disciple to go to the tomb. They ran together, but the other disciple, running faster than Peter, reached the tomb first; he bent down and saw the linen cloths lying on the ground, but did not go in. Simon Peter who was following now came up, went right into the tomb, saw the linen cloths on the ground, and also the cloth that had been over his head; this was not with the linen cloths but rolled up in a place by itself. Then the other disciple who had reached the tomb first also went in; he saw and he believed. Till this moment they had failed to understand the teaching of scripture, that he must rise from the dead.

EASTER SUNDAY

The Empty Tomb

Of the four accounts of the discovery of the empty tomb this account in the Gospel of John is chosen for the Easter Gospel because it is the most definite. The witnesses do not rely on the word of the young man in white garments or the angels, but actually investigate and give the evidence of what they saw. Even so, this is not the oldest or the most convincing evidence of the Resurrection of Jesus. That is provided by a very ancient tradition given in 1 Corinthians 15:3-5, where Paul quotes a passage he learnt by heart and passed on to others; it must have been firm in the tradition a mere twenty years after the Resurrection itself: the tomb was empty and the Risen Christ had appeared to specific numbers of the brothers.

The 'other disciple', who entered the tomb later, but came to belief earlier, appears in four passages of John: at the Last Supper, beside the cross, here and at the lakeside. Deliberately, he is never named; he has no definite face. This is the symbolic portrait of the disciple whom Jesus loves, who is present at the Eucharist, shares in the sufferings of the cross, recognises the Resurrection and will remain as guarantor of the tradition until Jesus comes again - any disciples whom Jesus loves.

Nevertheless, a woman, Mary Magdalene, has the honour of being the first herald of the Resurrection.

In the evening of that same day, the first day of the week, the doors were closed in the room where the disciples were, for fear of the Jews. Jesus came and stood among them. He said to them, 'Peace be with you,' and showed them his hands and his side. The disciples were filled with joy when they saw the Lord, and he said to them again, 'Peace be with you.

'As the Father sent me, so am I sending you.' After saying this he breathed on them and said: 'Receive the Holy Spirit. For those whose sins you forgive, they are forgiven; for those whose sins you retain, they are retained.'

Thomas, called the Twin, who was one of the Twelve, was not with them when Jesus came. When the disciples said, 'We have seen the Lord,' he answered, 'Unless I see the holes that the nails made in his hands and can put my finger into the holes they made, and unless I can put my hand into his side, I refuse to believe.' Eight days later the disciples were in the house again and Thomas was with them. The doors were closed, but Jesus came in and stood among them. 'Peace be with you,' he said. Then he spoke to Thomas, 'Put your finger here; look, here are my hands. Give me your hand; put it into my side. Doubt no longer but believe.' Thomas replied, 'My Lord and my God!'

Jesus said to him:
'You believe because you can see me.
Happy are those who have not seen and yet believe.'

Jesus in the Upper Room

This is the concluding passage of the Gospel according to John, for the conclusion to this passage makes it clear that chapter 21, the breakfast on the lakeside, is an addition - though possibly also by the same author. It is the only passage in the Gospels where Jesus is addressed fairly and squarely as 'Lord and God', though there are other passages which make the same claim in less overt language. It also prepares for the mission of the disciples. Firstly, it strengthens the evidence that the Risen Christ has a full bodily presence which can be not only seen but also touched. More importantly, it narrates the gift to the disciples of the Spirit of Jesus promised in the Last Supper discourse, the Spirit which will guide the community and lead it into all truth, thus enabling it to continue the mission on which the Father sent his Son.

The gift of authority, expressed by the opposites, 'forgive sin' and 'retain sin' is a Hebrew way of expressing total authority ('from the rising of the sun to its setting' means 'everywhere'; 'cannot tell their right from their left' means 'total ignorance'), but the central promise and the central purpose of the mission is peace, peace through the divine mercy and forgiveness brought by the message of Christ.

JOHN 21:1-14

Jesus showed himself again to the disciples. It was by the Sea of Tiberias, and it happened like this: Simon Peter, Thomas called the Twin, Nathanael from Cana in Galilee, the sons of Zebedee and two more of his disciples were together. Simon Peter said, 'I'm going fishing.' They replied, 'We'll come with you.' They went out and got into the boat but caught nothing that night.

It was light by now and there stood Jesus on the shore, though the disciples did not realise that it was Jesus. Jesus called out, 'Have you caught anything, friends?' And when they answered, 'No,' he said, 'Throw the net out to starboard and you'll find something.' So they dropped the net, and there were so many fish that they could not haul it in. The disciple Jesus loved said to Peter, 'It is the Lord.' At these words 'It is the Lord', Simon Peter, who had practically nothing on, wrapped his cloak round him and jumped into the water. The other disciples came on in the boat, towing the net and the fish; they were only about a hundred yards from land.

As soon as they came ashore they saw that there was some bread there, and a charcoal fire with fish cooking on it. Jesus said, 'Bring some of the fish you have just caught.' Simon Peter went aboard and dragged the net to the shore, full of big fish, one hundred and fifty-three of them; and in spite of there being so many the net was not broken. Jesus said to them, 'Come and have breakfast.' None of the disciples was bold enough to ask, 'Who are you?'; they knew quite well it was the Lord. Jesus then stepped forward, took the bread and gave it to them, and the same with the fish. This was the third time that Jesus showed himself to the disciples after rising from the dead.

(Longer form John 21:1-19)

THIRD SUNDAY OF EASTER

Christ Meets the Disciples at the Sea of Galilee

On the north shore of the Sea of Galilee, some 5km west of Capernaum, is a little Roman harbour, where seven warm springs flow into the Lake; the fish gather there in spring. Peter, the fisherman, would have known it was a good place for a catch, and it is the traditional place of this meeting with the Risen Christ. Despite Peter's enthusiastic leap into the sea, some hesitated, as in each of the meetings with the Risen Christ. Thomas did not believe it was Jesus. The disciples on the way to Emmaus did not recognise him. Some hesitated when Jesus met them on the mountain in Galilee. Was he somehow changed? Was there an aura surrounding him? A new sense of majesty and glory? At any rate he still retains the simplicity of cooking breakfast for them.

In this first meeting with Christ after his triple denial Peter is brought to a triple affirmation of his love for Jesus. He is amusingly nettled at the third question; is it a sign rather of confident and overflowing love rather than of annoyance? Only then is he given authority and care of the sheep. It is a useful reminder to any who bear authority in the Church that in the very act of receiving authority Peter was reminded of his previous falls and so of his fallibility. Furthermore, it leads Peter on to martyrdom, to going where he would rather not go, a further reminder that service brings sacrifice.

Jesus said:

> 'The sheep that belong to me listen to my voice;
> I know them and they follow me.
> I give them eternal life;
> they will never be lost
> and no one will ever steal them from me.
> The Father who gave them to me
> is greater than anyone,
> and no one can steal from the Father.
> The Father and I are one.'

The Good Shepherd

The image of Jesus as the Good Shepherd has a special importance. It is the nearest approach to a parable in the Gospel of John, and this is the only theological theme which is put before us by the Church in all three annual cycles of reading: the fourth Sunday of Easter is always Good Shepherd Sunday, and always uses John, chapter 10. The image of God as the shepherd has a long history, but reaches its Old Testament climax in Ezekiel 34, when the Lord condemns the slack and self-serving shepherds of Israel, promising to come and himself shepherd his flock. He and his Messiah, a second David, will be the shepherd - a single shepherd. So to proclaim the Risen Christ as the shepherd is tantamount to giving Jesus a divine title and role. The Messiah plays the part of God and is God's messenger and representative, so closely that it is often difficult to say whether the Messiah is God or only that God is at work in the Messiah. Before he feeds the five thousand, Jesus pities the people because they are like sheep without a shepherd.

Sheep are silly creatures, always running out in front of the car, having unnecessary panics, unable to make up their minds, getting caught in snares and fences, needing a fierce barking dog to keep them in order. The description fits most of us quite nicely! We certainly need the mercy of God.

When Judas had gone Jesus said:

'Now has the Son of Man been glorified,
and in him God has been glorified.
If God has been glorified in him,
God will in turn glorify him in himself,
and will glorify him very soon.
My little children,
I shall not be with you much longer.
I give you a new commandment:
love one another;
just as I have loved you,
you also must love one another.
By this love you have for one another,
everyone will know that you are my disciples.'

The Commandment of Love

From now until Pentecost the Gospel readings are taken from Jesus's Discourse after the Last Supper, the gathering of sayings about the future of the Church, placed at the Last Supper by John, forming a blueprint for the Church which will come into being with the coming of the Spirit at Pentecost. There seem to be three versions of these instructions: the present reading and following verses, chapters 15-16 and chapter 17. The first and principal instruction is that his followers should love one another. There is a lovely legend that the aged St John used to be carried into the church at Ephesus, where he was asked to give the message. All he would say was, 'Little children, love one another!'

The extent to which Christians have failed to implement this command of Christ and his Apostle is positively staggering. The Eastern and Western Churches split with mutual excommunications. In the fifteenth and sixteenth centuries Catholics and Protestants hanged and burnt one another over their doctrinal differences. Since then further chasms have occurred with such regularity that Christians take them for granted. Until recently and perhaps even today, the Roman Catholic Church has been one of the leaders in lack of love to those outside. Only recently has there been any serious attempt to discover how in good faith different groups can interpret their Christianity in so many ways. It is small wonder that so many non-Christians find simply ludicrous the Christian claim to follow a God of love.

Jesus said to his disciples:

'If anyone loves me he will keep my word,
and my Father will love him,
and we shall come to him
and make our home with him.
Those who do not love me do not keep my words.
And my word is not my own:
it is the word of the one who sent me.
I have said these things to you
while still with you;
but the Advocate, the Holy Spirit,
whom the Father will send in my name,
will teach you everything
and remind you of all I have said to you.
Peace I bequeath to you,
my own peace I give you,
a peace the world cannot give, this is my gift to you.
Do not let your hearts be troubled or afraid.
You heard me say:
I am going away, and shall return.
If you loved me you would have been glad to know
that I am going to the Father,
for the Father is greater than I.
I have told you this now before it happens,
so that when it does happen you may believe.'

The Promise of the Spirit

These instructions of Jesus at the Last Supper for the future of his community are shot through with assurances that he will be with them through the holy Spirit, a mysterious helper, a Paraclete whom the Father will send in his name. 'Paraclete' is a legal term, standing for a supporter, called to stand by a person in a lawsuit. The help brought by this Paraclete is described in four passages. The Paraclete will strengthen Jesus's disciples with Christ's own strength, will lead the disciples into all truth so that they gradually come to a fuller understanding of the implications of the teaching of Jesus and are enabled to put them into practice.

In Luke's terminology this links to the Spirit with which Jesus is filled in his mission, and which comes to the community at Pentecost to empower them for their mission. The only security of the Church, composed of human beings of more or less wisdom, more or less constancy, is the stability, power and wisdom of the Paraclete, dwelling not only in the ordained leaders of the Church but in every member of the Church. It is the Spirit who prays in every Christian, enlightens and guides our decisions, and enables us to carry out the work of Christ in all its wonder. The Paraclete enables us to restrain our human folly and selfishness and express in our words and deeds the love of God.

Jesus said to his disciples: 'You see how it is written that the Christ would suffer and on the third day rise from the dead, and that, in his name, repentance for the forgiveness of sins would be preached to all the nations, beginning from Jerusalem. You are witnesses to this.

'And now I am sending down to you what the Father has promised. Stay in the city then, until you are clothed with the power from on high.' Then he took them out as far as the outskirts of Bethany, and lifting up his hands he blessed them. Now as he blessed them, he withdrew from them and was carried up to heaven. They worshipped him and then went back to Jerusalem full of joy; and they were continually in the Temple praising God.

Departure of the Risen Christ

There is a lovely sense of completion in this account of the departure of the Risen Christ, and also a splendid sense of opening towards the future. The sense of completion comes from the return to the Temple: the Gospel began with Zachariah receiving in the Temple the promise of a son who would prepare the way for Jesus; it ends with the disciples in the Temple, thanking God and waiting for the next step in the story of salvation.

The sense of an opening to the future comes from the careful parallel with the departure of Elijah in the Book of Kings. Throughout the Gospel Jesus has been presented as a prophet ('a great prophet has risen among us, God has visited his people'), and now he goes up to heaven and is taken away by a divine cloud, just as the prophet Elijah went up to heaven in a fiery chariot. But the salient point is that Elisha caught Elijah's cloak as he went, and so continued his mission as his successor with a double share of his spirit. This is one of a series of succession-stories in the Bible, when one great leader is succeeded by another - Moses hands over to Joshua, Elijah to Elisha. So now, the disciples of Jesus will receive his Spirit to enable them to carry on his mission. The Church acts in the person of Christ, bringing Christ into the world for each new generation.

In the evening of the first day of the week, the doors were closed in the room where the disciples were, for fear of the Jews. Jesus came and stood among them. He said to them, 'Peace be with you,' and showed them his hands and his side. The disciples were filled with joy when they saw the Lord, and he said to them again, 'Peace be with you.

'As the Father sent me,
so am I sending you.'

After saying this he breathed on them and said:

'Receive the Holy Spirit.
For those whose sins you forgive,
they are forgiven;
for those whose sins you retain,
they are retained.'

The Gift of Peace

Naturally, there cannot be a Gospel reading about the descent of the Spirit at Pentecost, because this occurs after the departure of Jesus and the end of the Gospel: the Spirit comes to replace the physical presence of Jesus. The Gospel reading chosen therefore tells us of the gift of the spirit of peace and forgiveness from the Risen Christ. Just as in the Garden of Eden God breathed into the nostrils of Adam the spirit of life and of peace, so now Christ breathes into his timorous disciples the Spirit of new life and new peace.

This peace of the Spirit is to be not simply the absence of strife but a positive renewal of the peace and harmony of original innocence. Harmony is not silence, but is an agreeable web of sound. Friendship is not absence of enmity but is a positive and joyful partnership and exchange. So the original peace is not solitude (Adam could not have peace without Eve!) but is a welcoming web of relationships, bringing joy and happiness to anyone who encounters it. In our world, full of hazards and mistakes, this cannot occur without the mutual joy of forgiveness. So the Risen Christ gives the power of forgiveness, and also - let's be hard-nosed and realistic - the possibility of recognising that there is no desire for forgiveness.

Pentecost - alternative for Year C (John 14:15-16, 23-26)
The Paraclete. See commentary on Sixth Sunday of Easter.

Jesus said to his disciples:

> 'I still have many things to say to you
> but they would be too much for you now.
> But when the Spirit of truth comes
> he will lead you to the complete truth,
> since he will not be speaking as from himself
> but will say only what he has learnt;
> and he will tell you of the things to come.
> He will glorify me,
> since all he tells you
> will be taken from what is mine.
> Everything the Father has is mine;
> that is why I said:
> All he tells you
> will be taken from what is mine.'

THE MOST HOLY TRINITY

God the Father, Son and Holy Spirit

The doctrine of the Holy Trinity was elaborated long after the completion of the New Testament. With the aid of Greek philosophy some sort of explanation was worked out how we could speak of three separate entities which yet form one inseparable being. Questionable whether the definition of three persons in one nature is any clearer than the three-leafed clover traditionally used by St Patrick! If God is love, there must be love between what in inadequate human language we call persons. The Gospel reading chosen shows a loving harmony between Son, Father and Spirit, a Spirit which joins Father and Son together, but is sent by the Father just as the Son was sent by the Father. From other passages we know that the Father has given everything to the Son and that the Son does the will of the Father. In other passages we are told that the Father creates and works through the Son, that the Spirit or the Wisdom of God was the template of creation. These are all limping images which help us towards a veiled glimpse of what the Trinity might be. The only mistake is to imagine that we can understand the being of our Creator, our Redeemer and our Saviour. We can't really understand even what love is!

Jesus made the crowds welcome and talked to them about the kingdom of God; and he cured those who were in need of healing.

It was late afternoon when the Twelve came to him and said, 'Send the people away, and they can go to the villages and farms round about to find lodging and food; for we are in a lonely place here.' He replied, 'Give them something to eat yourselves.' But they said, 'We have no more than five loaves and two fish, unless we are to go ourselves and buy food for all these people.' For there were about five thousand men. But he said to his disciples, 'Get them to sit down in parties of about fifty.' They did so and made them all sit down. Then he took the five loaves and the two fish, raised his eyes to heaven, and said the blessing over them; then he broke them and handed them to his disciples to distribute among the crowd. They all ate as much as they wanted, and when the scraps remaining were collected they filled twelve baskets.

Jesus gives Food to the Crowds

This is Luke's version of the Feeding of the Five Thousand. In Luke the story has a slightly different point to the account in Mark and Matthew, for Luke omits the allusion to Jesus as the Good Shepherd feeding his sheep on green pastures. It comes immediately after the return of the disciples from their first missionary expedition - a sort of 'welcome back' meal, except that the crowds muscle in on it, and Jesus courteously makes them welcome. He welcomes all to his Eucharist. The preliminary is that, just as at the Eucharist, he first speaks to them about the Kingdom of God and then he heals all those who were in need of healing, for the Eucharist is always a celebration of listening and of healing. It is significant that the crowds provide almost nothing of their own, for we contribute only ourselves and our goodwill to the Eucharist. Knowing our need (it is a lonely place and there are no other resources), we come as healed sinners rather than as contributors to the meal provided by Jesus. The overtones of the Eucharist are unmistakable, in the way Jesus blesses the bread and hands it round. The disciples then hand it on, for they are already his intermediaries with the crowds. The twelve baskets of scraps, corresponding to the number of the tribes of Israel, is an indication that this is the meal of Jesus's New Israel.

Jesus went to a town called Nain, accompanied by his disciples and a great number of people. When he was near the gate of the town it happened that a dead man was being carried out for burial, the only son of his mother, and she was a widow. And a considerable number of the townspeople were with her. When the Lord saw her he felt sorry for her. 'Do not cry' he said. Then he went up and put his hand on the bier and the bearers stood still, and he said, 'Young man, I tell you to get up.' And the dead man sat up and began to talk, and Jesus gave him to his mother. Everyone was filled with awe and praised God saying, 'A great prophet has appeared among us; God has visited his people.' And this opinion of him spread throughout Judaea and all over the countryside.

The Son of the Widow of Nain

This story of the healing of the widow's son perfectly characterises the Jesus of Luke's Gospel. Jesus shows his perceptiveness and his sympathy. The young man was her only son, so she was now alone in the world, destitute and unable to support herself until Jesus perceives her need. As so often with the women depicted in the Gospels (the woman taken in adultery, the sinful woman who weeps at Jesus's feet), the approach of Jesus is straightforward. He does not question her or demand her faith; he knows that she is in need of his mercy, for her whole situation makes that clear, and he gives it directly.

Another typical feature of Luke's Gospel is that he is at pains to show the equality of men and women. The other synoptic Gospels relate the raising to life of Jairus's dead daughter; now Luke doubly reverses the sexes by inserting the raising to life of the widow's son. He frequently does the same: the annunciation of a son to Zechariah and to Mary, the prophet Simeon and the prophetess Anna, the man who finds his sheep and the woman who finds her coin, the sinful woman at Simon's house and the sinful man Zacchaeus.

Jesus is hailed as a prophet; 'God has visited his people.' The prophets heralded God's Kingdom, proclaimed that God would touch the world in mercy. Jesus already shows that touch of the world in mercy and healing.

One of the Pharisees invited Jesus to a meal. When he arrived at the Pharisee's house and took his place at table, a woman came in, who had a bad name in the town. She had heard he was dining with the Pharisee and had brought with her an alabaster jar of ointment. She waited behind him at his feet, weeping, and her tears fell on his feet, and she wiped them away with her hair; then she covered his feet with kisses and anointed them with the ointment.

When the Pharisee who had invited him saw this, he said to himself, 'If this man were a prophet, he would know who this woman is that is touching him and what a bad name she has.' Then Jesus took him up and said, 'Simon, I have something to say to you.' 'Speak, Master' was the reply. 'There was once a creditor who had two men in his debt; one owed him five hundred denarii, the other fifty. They were unable to pay, so he pardoned them both. Which of them will love him more?' 'The one who was pardoned more, I suppose' answered Simon. Jesus said, 'You are right.'

Then he turned to the woman. 'Simon,' he said 'you see this woman? I came into your house, and you poured no water over my feet, but she has poured out her tears over my feet and wiped them away with her hair. You gave me no kiss, but she has been covering my feet with kisses ever since I came in. You did not anoint my head with oil, but she has anointed my feet with ointment. For this reason I tell you that her sins, her many sins, must have been forgiven her, or she would not have shown such great love.

It is the man who is forgiven little who shows little love.' Then he said to her, 'Your sins are forgiven.' Those who were with him at table began to say to themselves, 'Who is this man, that he even forgives sins?' But he said to the woman, 'Your faith has saved you; go in peace.'

Longer form Luke 7:36-8:3

The Woman who was a Sinner

Again note the tact and gentleness of Jesus towards a woman. At a formal meal the diners would be reclining, supported on their left elbows, perhaps at a horseshoe-shaped low table. She takes a humble position behind him. The feet of an itinerant teacher, grimed with sand and dust of the roads, are not the most attractive; Jesus had had no chance to wash them, for Simon had not given him the welcoming courtesy of water or greeting. He does not interrogate her, ask why she is distressed or why she comes to him weeping and pouring out her expensive gift. He cares nothing for her dubious reputation, but accepts her as she presents herself - in a tender outpouring of affection.

The contrast with Simon is blatant, for the Pharisees above all were respected for their exact observance of Law both oral and written. No doubt Simon reckoned that his observance was perfect - but at least his hospitality was lacking: perhaps the requirements of the Law had been fulfilled, but not those of human courtesy and affection.

There is a slight logical problem: the woman's action shows great love and appears to earn her forgiveness. But the verbal exchange (especially Jesus's summing up: 'one to whom little is forgiven loves little') is based on the premise that love follows forgiveness, and great love is the result, rather than the cause, of great forgiveness.

One day when Jesus was praying alone in the presence of his disciples he put this question to them, 'Who do the crowds say I am?' And they answered, 'John the Baptist; others Elijah; and others say one of the ancient prophets come back to life.' 'But you,' he said 'who do you say I am?' It was Peter who spoke up. 'The Christ of God' he said. But he gave them strict orders not to tell anyone anything about this.

'The Son of Man' he said 'is destined to suffer grievously, to be rejected by the elders and chief priests and scribes and to be put to death, and to be raised up on the third day.'

Then to all he said, 'If anyone wants to be a follower of mine, let him renounce himself and take up his cross every day and follow me. For anyone who wants to save his life will lose it; but anyone who loses his life for my sake, that man will save it.'

Peter Acknowledges Jesus as Messiah

Peter's sudden insight is a turning-point in the Gospel. To us, who from the beginning of Jesus's ministry (the descent of the Spirit on him at his baptism and the Voice from heaven) have known who he is, the disciples seem infuriatingly slow to realise that he is the Messiah. Time and again, especially in the Gospel of Mark, they have been corrected and prodded, 'Do you still not realise, still not understand?' The answers given at the beginning of this passage show that there was a feeling around that Jesus was something special and mysterious, but Peter's insight comes as a thunderbolt. To us, who are used to the idea that Jesus is the Messiah, it does not seem so staggering, but at the time it was breath-taking: 'You are the climax of all history. You are the fulfilment of everything anyone ever hoped for.'

But the more difficult step is still to come. The climax of all history was not to be star-studded glory and celebration. Jesus chided them and began to try to convince them that before being raised on the third day (and what could that mean?) he must suffer and be despised and rejected. Three times he drums in this lesson, and each time they misunderstand it. To make matters worse, he says to them all that anyone who wants to be a follower of his must take up the cross every day. No, actually he says it not to 'them all', but to 'all'. Does that include me?

As the time drew near for him to be taken up to heaven, Jesus resolutely took the road for Jerusalem and sent messengers ahead of him. These set out, and they went into a Samaritan village to make preparations for him, but the people would not receive him because he was making for Jerusalem. Seeing this, the disciples James and John said, 'Lord, do you want us to call down fire from heaven to burn them up?' But he turned and rebuked them, and they went off to another village.

As they travelled along they met a man on the road who said to him, 'I will follow you wherever you go.' Jesus answered, 'Foxes have holes and the birds of the air have nests, but the Son of Man has nowhere to lay his head.'

Another to whom he said, 'Follow me,' replied, 'Let me go and bury my father first.' But he answered, 'Leave the dead to bury their dead; your duty is to go and spread the news of the kingdom of God.'

Another said, 'I will follow you, sir, but first let me go and say good-bye to my people at home.' Jesus said to him, 'Once the hand is laid on the plough, no one who looks back is fit for the kingdom of God.'

Uncompromising Discipleship

Jesus now sets his face towards Jerusalem, going up to the city for his final sacrifice. On the journey up, as related by Luke, the disciples are told in one story after another of all the difficulties of following Jesus and being his disciple. Particularly in this first passage the demands of Jesus are fierce and uncompromising. One after another come the volleys. First there comes a bland and enthusiastic offer to follow Jesus anywhere - to be met by an uncompromising challenge that this means total homelessness and giving up all treasured possessions. Then another volunteer, but he must first bury his dead father. In Judaism this is an especially sacred duty - but no, not even this may stand in the way of discipleship. Then comes a third, who wants first to bid the family farewell - but following Jesus annihilates all normal family and social obligations. These three hammer-blows are capped by the image of the plough: if you set your hand to the plough and look back you are not fit for the Kingdom. A moment's distraction from a Palestinian hand-plough, a single glance behind you, and all is lost.

Must every follower of Jesus be destitute and homeless? Perhaps not literally, but the demands of Jesus leave no room for half-measures. The decision must be made, as Jesus will later say to Martha and Mary, that one thing alone is necessary, and no human tie must be allowed to stand in its way.

The Lord appointed seventy-two others and sent them out ahead of him, in pairs, to all the towns and places he himself was to visit. He said to them, 'The harvest is rich but the labourers are few, so ask the Lord of the harvest to send labourers to his harvest. Start off now, but remember, I am sending you out like lambs among wolves. Carry no purse, no haversack, no sandals. Salute no one on the road. Whatever house you go into, let your first words be, "Peace to this house!" And if a man of peace lives there, your peace will go and rest on him; if not, it will come back to you. Stay in the same house, taking what food and drink they have to offer, for the labourer deserves his wages; do not move from house to house. Whenever you go into a town where they make you welcome, eat what is set before you. Cure those in it who are sick, and say, "The kingdom of God is very near to you."

A Healing Mission

At the beginning of this journey up to Jerusalem Jesus has made it clear that no human tie must stand in the way. Now he follows it up: the journey itself must be unyielding, as unprotected as sheep among wolves. No money, no spares, no choice of food or lodging, no greeting on the road. Their task is only to proclaim the urgency of the Kingship of God and to heal all those in need of healing.

Do we all have to work miracles? Yes, we live in a wounded world and are ourselves wounded. Jesus is not speaking only of physical healing but of the healing which we can all bring to others. Does a day ever pass of which I can say in the evening that I have brought healing to everyone I met, or even that I have tried to bring such healing? To everyone? This does not mean being soft and supine, for healing requires skill and firmness. But above all it needs love, respect and care, a real commitment to the person I meet. We do not doubt the love of Jesus for ourselves, and yet the path down which he leads us is not primroses all the way. If we want to avoid hypocrisy in our pursuit of the Kingship of God we need first of all the patience and wisdom to act in the image of God and the imitation of Christ. Then we can touch the mercy of God, and miracles will start happening.

There was a lawyer who, to disconcert Jesus, stood up and said to him, 'Master, what must I do to inherit eternal life?' He said to him, 'What is written in the law? What do you read there?' He replied, 'You must love the Lord your God with all your heart, with all your soul, with all your strength, and with all your mind, and your neighbour as yourself.' 'You have answered right,' said Jesus 'do this and life is yours.'

But the man was anxious to justify himself and said to Jesus, 'And who is my neighbour?' Jesus replied, 'A man was once on his way down from Jerusalem to Jericho and fell into the hands of brigands; they took all he had, beat him and then made off, leaving him half dead. Now a priest happened to be travelling down the same road, but when he saw the man, he passed by on the other side. In the same way a Levite who came to the place saw him, and passed by on the other side. But a Samaritan traveller who came upon him was moved with compassion when he saw him. He went up and bandaged his wounds, pouring oil and wine on them. He then lifted him on to his own mount, carried him to the inn and looked after him. Next day, he took out two denarii and handed them to the innkeeper. "Look after him," he said "and on my way back I will make good any extra expense you have." Which of these three, do you think, proved himself a neighbour to the man who fell into the brigands' hands?' 'The one who took pity on him' he replied. Jesus said to him, 'Go, and do the same yourself.'

The Good Samaritan

The path from Jerusalem to Jericho lies in a dangerous canyon, with high rocky walls and a twisting river-bed, which is dry for most of the year. It is still possible to walk there without seeing anyone for a couple of hours or more. So it is ideal for an ambush by bandits: no cover, no escape, no shouting for help.

There are many layers to this story and a good deal of underlying humour. It is not simply that the Jews hated and despised the Samaritans and would have difficulty in accepting that a Samaritan would do such a good deed which two Jews (and two Jews dedicated to the service of God) failed to do. The two Temple officials were faced with a problem: if the crumpled figure lying there is dead, they will be defiled by touching him, and so unable to perform their sacred duties that day. Should they observe the Law or give help where help is needed? The Samaritan has no such worry and takes the injured man as his neighbour. Yet he remains shrewd, handing over only a couple of days' wages; on his return he will be able to demand an account for the excess! There is no doubt who is the more attractive person in human terms, as even the lawyer who put the question must admit. In this case the Law is no help to serving a neighbour.

Jesus came to a village, and a woman named Martha welcomed him into her house. She had a sister called Mary, who sat down at the Lord's feet and listened to him speaking. Now Martha who was distracted with all the serving said, 'Lord, do you not care that my sister is leaving me to do the serving all by myself? Please tell her to help me.' But the Lord answered 'Martha, Martha,' he said 'you worry and fret about so many things, and yet few are needed, indeed only one. It is Mary who has chosen the better part; it is not to be taken from her.'

Martha and Mary

The Good Samaritan illustrated the second commandment of the Law, to love your neighbour as yourself; this next story now illustrates the first, to love God above all things. As always, Luke's characterisation of the sisterly rivalry is superb: Martha does not chide her sister directly, but goes around it through Jesus. The two appear again in the story of the raising of their brother Lazarus, where their affection for each other is more tangible.

They have become the classic figures of the active and contemplative life respectively. Martha fusses around about the practical details of serving the Lord, while Mary listens to him in peace and tranquillity. The two are sisters, and of course in reality there must be a blending of the two ways of life. The active life of pastoral care, teaching or visiting the sick, and all the other activities to which religious people devote themselves, cannot thrive unless it grows out of a life of prayer. On the other hand, nor does a life of fervent prayer ring true if it does not issue in care and concern for the elderly, the sick and the young.

Jesus does not resolve the question which is better. The Hebrew language does not favour comparatives. He says that Mary has chosen not the 'better' but the 'good' part, and that is enough.

Once Jesus was in a certain place praying, and when he had finished, one of his disciples said, 'Lord, teach us to pray, just as John taught his disciples.' He said to them, 'Say this when you pray:

> "Father, may your name be held holy,
> your kingdom come;
> give us each day our daily bread,
> and forgive us our sins,
> for we ourselves forgive each one who is in debt to us.
> And do not put us to the test."'

He also said to them, 'Suppose one of you has a friend and goes to him in the middle of the night to say, "My friend, lend me three loaves, because a friend of mine on his travels has just arrived at my house and I have nothing to offer him"; and the man answers from inside the house, "Do not bother me. The door is bolted now, and my children and I are in bed; I cannot get up to give it to you." I tell you, if the man does not get up and give it him for friendship's sake, persistence will be enough to make him get up and give his friend all he wants.

'So I say to you: Ask, and it will be given to you; search, and you will find; knock, and the door will be opened to you. For the one who asks always receives; the one who searches always finds; the one who knocks will always have the door opened to him. What father among you would hand his son a stone when he asked for bread? Or hand him a snake instead of a fish? Or hand him a scorpion if he asked for an egg? If you then, who are evil, know how to give your children what is good, how much more will the heavenly Father give the Holy Spirit to those who ask him!'

The Lord's Prayer

Luke's version of the Lord's Prayer is slightly different from the more familiar version of Matthew's Gospel, which we normally recite; it is simpler, which in some ways is more attractive. Which is the original version is hard (and unnecessary) to decide. To begin with, Luke's version starts with a simple cry, 'Father', instead of 'Our Father in heaven'. I like that simplicity and directness, though Matthew's 'Our' does remind us that we pray as a community.

Matthew has three petitions about God's business in the first half, followed by three in the second half about our cares and concerns. Luke has only two petitions in the first half, and perhaps the second half also counts as two petitions. In the first half Luke does not mention 'thy will be done' (actually doing God's will is a frequent concern of Matthew), and in the second half does not mention the Evil One. This focuses attention in the first half on God's Kingship. That God should truly be treated and revered as King by all people is really all our desire; there would then be perfect peace and happiness, and all would be open to God's boundless mercy. In the second half the focus is on forgiveness: we, for our part, want to put ourselves in God's merciful hands, and realise that we cannot hope to receive God's mercy unless we put ourselves in the same frame of mind that we wish to beam upon ourselves.

A man in the crowd said to Jesus, 'Master, tell my brother to give me a share of our inheritance.' 'My friend,' he replied, 'who appointed me your judge, or the arbitrator of your claims?' Then he said to them, 'Watch, and be on your guard against avarice of any kind, for a man's life is not made secure by what he owns, even when he has more than he needs.'

Then he told them a parable: 'There was once a rich man who, having had a good harvest from his land, thought to himself, "What am I to do? I have not enough room to store my crops." Then he said, "This is what I will do: I will pull down my barns and build bigger ones, and store all my grain and my goods in them, and I will say to my soul: My soul, you have plenty of good things laid by for many years to come; take things easy, eat, drink, have a good time." But God said to him, "Fool! This very night the demand will be made for your soul; and this hoard of yours, whose will it be then?" So it is when a man stores up treasure for himself in place of making himself rich in the sight of God.'

The Rich Fool

By contrast to Matthew and especially to Mark, Luke is writing for people in an easy financial situation. He uses larger sums of money; he is at home in a world of investment banking and rates of interest. Consequently he stresses more than the other evangelists the dangers of wealth, the opposing fates of the Rich Man and Lazarus, the distractions of possessions which keep the invited guests from attending the Great Supper (and they are pretty glib, too, with the icy politeness of their excuses!). The message of salvation comes first to the impoverished shepherds of Bethlehem, who have no sheep of their own, about a new-born baby cradled in a cattle-trough. Only in Luke are the apostles told they must leave 'everything' to follow Jesus. The only hope for the wealthy is to use their wealth to make themselves friends in heaven.

The parable of the Rich Fool is vivid in the extreme. It is also typical of Luke's style, with the chief character debating with himself what he should do next (so also the Prodigal Son, the Unjust Judge, the Dishonest Steward). Nowhere else in the Gospels is anyone called blatantly 'Fool' outright. His self-centredness is itself richly presented, '*my* harvest', '*my* barns', '*my* good things', 'I shall,...I shall,...I shall'. In the Acts of the Apostles we see the reverse of this attitude in the early Christian community, where they held all things in common and distributed to each according to need.

Jesus said to his disciples:

'See that you are dressed for action and have your lamps lit. Be like men waiting for their master to return from the wedding feast, ready to open the door as soon as he comes and knocks. Happy those servants whom the master finds awake when he comes. I tell you solemnly, he will put on an apron, sit them down at table and wait on them. It may be in the second watch he comes, or in the third, but happy those servants if he finds them ready. You may be quite sure of this, that if the householder had known at what hour the burglar would come, he would not have let anyone break through the wall of his house. You too must stand ready, because the Son of Man is coming at an hour you do not expect.'

(Longer form Luke 12:32-48)

The Return of the Master

This Gospel reading is looking towards the end. Luke has no grand judgement scene like Matthew's Sheep and Goats at the right and left of Christ enthroned in Judgement. In the Hellenistic manner, he is more concerned with the fate of each individual than with that of the universe as a whole. He envisages the moment of the individual, confronted with the Lord in the very moment of death. The three parables here are enveloped by a little encouragement at the beginning and a dire warning at the end.

The encouragement at the beginning is that we have no need of our possessions. Holes are worn and possessions are stolen, but our hearts should rely on the secure generosity of God. Then the most startling parable is the first: the Master when he comes will actually reverse roles, put on an apron and serve whoever is ready. Jesus will act out this parable at the Last supper, when he washes the disciples' feet. The second parable gives the other side of the coin: if you are not ready, the thief may dig through the wall unnoticed - obviously a Palestinian house built of mud-brick is envisaged. The third parable gives a pair of opposites, which seem to be a more succinct version of the parable of the talents which Luke will narrate later (19:12-27). Only now the unsatisfactory servant is not merely supine but positively misbehaves and makes mayhem in the household.

Jesus said to his disciples: 'I have come to bring fire to the earth, and how I wish it were blazing already! There is a baptism I must still receive, and how great is my distress till it is over!

'Do you suppose that I am here to bring peace on earth? No, I tell you, but rather division. For from now on a household of five will be divided: three against two and two against three; the father divided against the son, son against father, mother against daughter, daughter against mother, mother-in-law against daughter-in-law, daughter-in-law against mother-in-law.'

A Blazing Fire

This passage is a rude shock! 'You think that I have come to bring peace to the earth' Yes, we do indeed, and the Gospel has said so right from the beginning: 'Peace on earth, good will among men'. Now the reverse seems to be the case. Jesus can be rough and extreme in his statements and demands: 'Let the dead bury their dead', 'If your hand causes you to fall, cut it off', 'Such a one would be better off cast into the sea with a millstone round the neck'. Now he speaks of dissension within the family. But the family is the basic unit of society, where they have got to have you if you want to go home, the one place where you can be sure to find acceptance, a unit especially loving and united within Judaism.

Jesus deliberately takes the most sacred human bonds to show that loyalty to him transcends even that. The break-up of a family is the most tragic collapse of all, to be avoided at all costs - or nearly all. The mention of the 'baptism' with which Jesus is to be baptised is elsewhere paired with the cup which Jesus must drink, namely the Passion and Crucifixion. The sons of Zebedee are asked if they too are prepared to drink the cup, to undergo martyrdom. This suggests that Jesus and Luke are envisaging the situation of persecution in the first years of the Church. If one family member fails, the others must still hold fast in their loyalty to Christ.

Through towns and villages Jesus went teaching, making his way to Jerusalem. Someone said to him, 'Sir, will there be only a few saved?' He said to them, 'Try your best to enter by the narrow door, because, I tell you, many will try to enter and will not succeed.

'Once the master of the house has got up and locked the door, you may find yourself knocking on the door, saying, "Lord, open to us" but he will answer, "I do not know where you come from." Then you will find yourself saying, "We once ate and drank in your company; you taught in our streets" but he will reply, "I do not know where you come from. Away from me, all you wicked men!"

'Then there will be weeping and grinding of teeth, when you see Abraham and Isaac and Jacob and all the prophets in the kingdom of God, and yourselves turned outside. And men from east and west, from north and south, will come to take their places at the feast in the kingdom of God.

'Yes, there are those now last who will be first, and those now first who will be last.'

The Narrow Door

Luke is the evangelist for the gentiles, anxious on many occasions to underline that Jesus's offer of salvation is not merely for the Jews but for all nations. So much is clear from Simeon's 'light to enlighten the gentiles' and from Jesus's programmatic speech in the synagogue at Nazareth. This is one of the principal concerns of the Gospel. But the corollary contains a threat: will Simeon's 'for the glory of your people Israel' be fulfilled? In the first two chapters of Luke it is plain that salvation has come to Israel, or at any rate to those of Israel who trust in the Lord.

The present passage, with its knocking on the closed door, is markedly similar to Matthew's parable about the wedding attendants, some of whom have to go off and buy oil for their lamps and arrive too late for the wedding-feast. Possibly Matthew, with his preference for contrast-parables (house built on rock or on sand, narrow gate and broad road, children refusing to dance or to mourn) has built up this simple entry into a house into a messianic wedding-feast, and added the contrast of the well-prepared attendants.

Do we, however, have the same problem as Jews at the time of Jesus, who were so confident of their election that they assumed their entry into God's house was assured, and risked finding themselves altogether shut out?

On a sabbath day Jesus had gone for a meal to the house of one of the leading Pharisees; and they watched him closely. He then told the guests a parable, because he had noticed how they picked the places of honour. He said this, 'When someone invites you to a wedding feast, do not take your seat in the place of honour. A more distinguished person than you may have been invited, and the person who invited you both may come and say, "Give up your place to this man." And then, to your embarrassment, you would have to go and take the lowest place. No; when you are a guest, make your way to the lowest place and sit there, so that, when your host comes, he may say, "My friend, move up higher." In that way, everyone with you at the table will see you honoured. For everyone who exalts himself will be humbled, and the man who humbles himself will be exalted.'

Then he said to his host, 'When you give a lunch or a dinner, do not ask your friends, brothers, relations or rich neighbours, for fear they repay your courtesy by inviting you in return. No; when you have a party, invite the poor, the crippled, the lame, the blind; that they cannot pay you back means that you are fortunate, because repayment will be made to you when the virtuous rise again.'

Invitations to Dinner

From Luke's own special material, unparalleled in the other Gospels, come two pieces of advice about dinner invitations. Courtesy, good manners and avoidance of embarrassment are also Christian virtues, important in Luke's cosmopolitan environment. The first is founded on a proverb from the Old Testament, 'Do not give yourself airs, do not take a place among the great; better to be invited, "Come up here", than to be humiliated' (*Pr* 25:6-7). For Luke a banquet is always a foretaste of the heavenly marriage-feast, and a due sense of one's own limitations is always advantageous. The rank-order at the heavenly banquet may come as a surprise: beggars may come before bishops and prostitutes before popes!

The second piece of advice is also typical of Luke: he applies to the situation of every day Jesus's own teaching and behaviour to the poor, the outcast and the neglected in society. This teaching is then illustrated by the parable of the Great Feast: there the host invites the poor, the crippled, the blind and the lame, and then crams in the down-and-outs of the countryside. Perhaps in this day and age more important than financial and social considerations is concern for the lonely, the unwanted and the unpopular. Thomas More prayed fervently that he might meet his gaolers and tormentors in heaven; perhaps we should prepare ourselves even now by setting about learning the attractive features of those on the margins of our society.

Great crowds accompanied Jesus on his way and he turned and spoke to them. 'If any man comes to me without hating his father, mother, wife, children, brothers, sisters, yes and his own life too, he cannot be my disciple. Anyone who does not carry his cross and come after me cannot be my disciple.

'And indeed, which of you here, intending to build a tower, would not first sit down and work out the cost to see if he had enough to complete it? Otherwise, if he laid the foundation and then found himself unable to finish the work, the onlookers would all start making fun of him and saying, "Here is a man who started to build and was unable to finish." Or again, what king marching to war against another king would not first sit down and consider whether with ten thousand men he could stand up to the other who advanced against him with twenty thousand? If not, then while the other king was still a long way off, he would send envoys to sue for peace. So in the same way, none of you can be my disciple unless he gives up all his possessions.'

The Cost of Discipleship

The underlying theme of the whole of this section of the Gospel is the cost of discipleship, but none is more uncompromising than this passage. Must the disciple really hate father, mother and all the family? Must the disciple really give up 'all his possessions'? Elsewhere, must disciple really cut off hand, foot, eye if they offend? Is it really harder for the rich to be saved than for a camel to pass through the eye of a needle?

Two slight mitigations might be considered. Luke does insist that the disciple must leave *all* possessions, both here and in the call of the first disciples (5:11) and of Levi (5:28). In the Acts of the Apostles all possessions are held in common (2:44). But when Ananias lies over the total generosity of his gift, Peter judges him for the lie rather than for withholding money, which suggests that he could have held at least some of it back (*Ac* 5:4). Another plea may be entered, a literary one: the Hebrew language and the language of Jesus do not encourage comparatives: it is either 'good' or 'bad', not 'better' or 'worse'. This is exemplified in Matthew's stark contrasts between characters: Luke's rogues are often puzzlingly attractive, doing the right thing for the wrong reason, but Matthew's are either sheep or goats.

Nevertheless, the demands of Jesus are stark and absolute. Discipleship is not to be lightly undertaken; there is no escaping the cost.

The tax collectors and the sinners were all seeking the company of Jesus to hear what he had to say, and the Pharisees and the scribes complained. 'This man' they said 'welcomes sinners and eats with them.' So he spoke this parable to them:

'What man among you with a hundred sheep, losing one, would not leave the ninety-nine in the wilderness and go after the missing one till he found it? And when he found it, would he not joyfully take it on his shoulders and then, when he got home, call together his friends, and neighbours? "Rejoice with me," he would say "I have found my sheep that was lost." In the same way, I tell you, there will be more rejoicing in heaven over one repentant sinner than over ninety-nine virtuous men who have no need of repentance.

'Or again, what woman with ten drachmas would not, if she lost one, light a lamp and sweep out the house and search thoroughly till she found it? And then, when she had found it, call together her friends and neighbours? "Rejoice with me," she would say "I have found the drachma I lost." In the same way, I tell you, there is rejoicing among the angels of God over one repentant sinner.'

(Longer form Luke 15:1-32)

Forgiveness

Here is the divine mercy at its most explicit, the joy in heaven at one repentant sinner. First Luke applies this by gender stereotype, the man a devoted shepherd and the woman a careful housekeeper. Her house would not have the luxury of windows; she has to sweep the earth floor by the light from the doorway. Then that beloved parable of the Prodigal Son. The rascal insults his father by grabbing the cash before the father is even dead, defiles himself by working for unclean masters in an unclean land with unclean pigs. Then he goes home with his (fairly) pretty speech about hunger - not a sign of apology, let alone repayment, only a smidgeon of humility! The father, straining his eyes in hope, breaks into an undignified run and cuts short the (fairly) pretty speech and lavishes everything on the wastrel. A fatted calf would feed the whole village. Then, to make quite sure that the listeners' sympathy is firmly with the re-united pair, the supposedly dutiful son turns out to be rude, vengeful, unfraternal and stubborn, dead set on ruining the home-coming party.

The parable has all the charm of a Lukan parable: the mixed characters, doing the right thing for the wrong reason, the puzzled self-questioning of the 'hero' (or anti-hero), the lively dialogue, but above all the unconditional love and welcome from the Father.

Jesus said to his disciples: 'There was a rich man and he had a steward who was denounced to him for being wasteful with his property. He called for the man and said, "What is this I hear about you? Draw me up an account of your stewardship because you are not to be my steward any longer." Then the steward said to himself, "Now that my master is taking the stewardship from me, what am I to do? Dig? I am not strong enough. Go begging? I should be too ashamed. Ah, I know what I will do to make sure that when I am dismissed from office there will be some to welcome me into their homes."

'Then he called his master's debtors one by one. To the first he said, "How much do you owe my master?" "One hundred measures of oil" was the reply. The steward said, "Here, take your bond; sit down straight away and write fifty." To another he said, "And you, sir, how much do you owe?" "One hundred measures of wheat" was the reply. The steward said, "Here, take your bond and write eighty."

'The master praised the dishonest steward for his astuteness. For the children of this world are more astute in dealing with their own kind than are the children of light.

'And so I tell you this: use money, tainted as it is, to win you friends, and thus make sure that when it fails you, they will welcome you into the tents of eternity. The man who can be trusted in little things can be trusted in great; the man who is dishonest in little things will be dishonest in great. If then you cannot be trusted with money, that tainted thing, who will trust you with genuine riches? And if you cannot be trusted with what is not yours, who will give you what is your very own?

'No servant can be the slave of two masters: he will either hate the first and love the second, or treat the first with respect and the second with scorn. You cannot be the slave both of God and of money.'

The Dishonest Steward

This intriguing parable must not be taken as an allegory. In an allegory there is a point-by-point equivalent for every element; so in the parables of the wheat and the weed each object in the story has its meaning in the moral (farmer, wheat, weed, harvest, reapers). For a parable only one lesson, one comparison is needed. If we take this parable as an allegory we have God praising the steward for his dishonesty! The one lesson is the energy and inventiveness with which the steward sets about securing his future, exceeding the energy with which we pursue our religious and spiritual objectives. Only too true! We often tend to leave God's business to God: 'God can swing this if he wants, so there is no need for me to help.'

Why the difference between bills for corn and oil? This gives a neat little twist to the story. It seems to have been standard to lend oil at a higher rate of interest than corn. If I pay back a sack of corn, which in fact is well adulterated with chaff, this can be easily and quickly discovered by a mere riffle of the hand. If I pay back a can of olive oil which has been adulterated with sesame oil, this is not so easy or so quick to detect. So the steward is in fact cutting off the interest on the loans. The master cannot complain, because the Jewish Law forbids lending at interest to other Jews; he is only being brought back into line with the Law!

Jesus said to the Pharisees: 'There was a rich man who used to dress in purple and fine linen and feast magnificently everyday. And at his gate there lay a poor man called Lazarus, covered with sores, who longed to fill himself with the scraps that fell from the rich man's table. Dogs even came and licked his sores. Now the poor man died and was carried away by the angels to the bosom of Abraham. The rich man also died and was buried.

'In his torment in Hades he looked up and saw Abraham a long way off with Lazarus in his bosom. So he cried out, "Father Abraham, pity me and send Lazarus to dip the tip of his finger in water and cool my tongue, for I am in agony in these flames." "My son," Abraham replied "remember that during your life good things came your way, just as bad things came the way of Lazarus. Now he is being comforted here while you are in agony. But that is not all: between us and you a great gulf has been fixed, to stop anyone, if he wanted to, crossing from our side to yours, and to stop any crossing from your side to ours."

'The rich man replied, "Father, I beg you then to send Lazarus to my father's house, since I have five brothers, to give them warning so that they do not come to this place of torment too." "They have Moses and the prophets," said Abraham "let them listen to them." "Ah no, father Abraham," said the rich man "but if someone comes to them from the dead, they will repent." Then Abraham said to him, "If they will not listen either to Moses or to the prophets, they will not be convinced even if someone should rise from the dead."'

The Rich Man and Lazarus

There has been plenty of teaching in Luke contrasting the fate of the rich and of the poor. In the Infancy Narratives the blessing is all on the poor and unfortunate (childless old people, impoverished shepherds). Most striking is Luke's version of the Beatitudes: instead of Matthew's eight blessings for various Christian frames of mind and motivations, Luke give us four blessings on those who are materially poor, followed by four corresponding 'Woes' on the rich and comfortable. In Matthew's Last Judgement scene a favourable verdict is won by thoughtfulness and attention to the poor and neglected. Here, in this story, it is simply the status of utter poverty which wins a reward. Perhaps the single most colourful detail is the dogs licking Lazarus's sores. This is not a charming partnership with animals; it is simply the depth of disgust. There are no pets in Palestine. Dogs are either fierce guardians or flea-ridden scavengers. Similarly the Rich Man is not represented as immoral; his trouble is simply his purple and fine linen, his daily dinner-parties and his grand gateway. He does have the decency to be worried about his own brothers.

The tragedy is that Abraham (with the Poor Man nestling in his lap) simply cannot help. He is quite sympathetic, and even calls the Rich Man 'My son', but by then no remedy is possible. It is simply very dangerous to be rich and not use the wealth while there is a chance of making friends in heaven.

The apostles said to the Lord, 'Increase our faith.' The Lord replied, 'Were your faith the size of a mustard seed you could say to this mulberry tree, "Be uprooted and planted in the sea," and it would obey you.

'Which of you, with a servant ploughing or minding sheep, would say to him when he returned from the fields, "Come and have your meal immediately"? Would he not be more likely to say, "Get my supper laid; make yourself tidy and wait on me while I eat and drink. You can eat and drink yourself afterwards"? Must he be grateful to the servant for doing what he was told? So with you: when you have done all you have been told to do, say, "We are merely servants: we have done no more than our duty."'

The Reward of Faith

At first sight the two themes of this little passage seem entirely unrelated, the need for faith and the strict and unyielding behaviour of the slave-owner. But it is of the very nature of faith that it involves perseverance and patience.

The first image of the mulberry tree is surely meant to be absurd. Jesus sometimes has a way of stating his point in a way which seems to us exaggerated! Cutting off a hand or foot which offends is surely not Jesus's literal intention. The rich are not excluded from the Kingdom of God quite as strictly as the camel from passing through the eye of a needle; this is only a way of issuing a dauntingly strong warning. In the same way, the image of the mulberry tree is only a way of stating with maximum strength that there is nothing that faith cannot achieve.

It is important to remember that not all parables are allegories. The difference is that in an allegory each point of the story has a meaning of its own (as in the parable of the wheat and the weeds), whereas in a parable it is necessary to have only one point of comparison. So we need not think of God as the severe and unappreciative slave-owner who comes home and demands his dinner from the already exhausted slave. The point of the parable is the need for endurance if we are to serve God as he should be served.

On the way to Jerusalem Jesus travelled along the border between Samaria and Galilee. As he entered one of the villages, ten lepers came to meet him. They stood some way off and called to him, 'Jesus! Master! Take pity on us.' When he saw them he said, 'Go and show yourselves to the priests.' Now as they were going away they were cleansed. Finding himself cured, one of them turned back praising God at the top of his voice and threw himself at the feet of Jesus and thanked him. The man was a Samaritan. This made Jesus say, 'Were not all ten made clean? The other nine, where are they? It seems that no one has come back to give praise to God, except this foreigner.' And he said to the man, 'Stand up and go on your way. Your faith has saved you.'

The Samaritan Leper

Leprosy was a term wider than the modern meaning given to it, for the Book of Leviticus speaks also of the leprosy of walls - what we would now call the effect of damp. So in humans it embraces several other contagious sin diseases. However, it certainly entailed isolation from the community. Luke's main point is the importance of gratitude to God, which he frequently calls 'praising' or 'glorifying God', for that is what gratitude to God is.

He is also preparing for the mission to the gentiles in the Acts of the Apostles, when the message of the Gospel will be carried far and wide to the gentiles. They will respond better than the Jews. The Samaritans were especially despised by the Jews, being near neighbours and holding some of the same beliefs in what the Jews regarded as an ignorant and distorted way. They were of mixed race and mixed religions. In any case, neighbours are often the most highly criticised!

Being the Chosen Race was a dangerous situation, and the Jews are often criticised in the Bible for assuming that they alone are to be saved, for example in the Book of Jonah, where Jonah is the fall-guy and runs away, while the inhabitants of wicked city Nineveh repent enthusiastically as soon as he preaches to them. Similarly, it is easy for Christians to be blind to the generosity and responsiveness of the non-Christians who surround us.

Jesus told his disciples a parable about the need to pray continually and never lose heart. 'There was a judge in a certain town' he said 'who had neither fear of God nor respect for man. In the same town there was a widow who kept on coming to him and saying, "I want justice from you against my enemy!" For a long time he refused, but at last he said to himself, "Maybe I have neither fear of God nor respect for man, but since she keeps pestering me I must give this widow her just rights, or she will persist in coming and worry me to death."'

And the Lord said, 'You notice what the unjust judge has to say? Now will not God see justice done to his chosen who cry to him day and night even when he delays to help them? I promise you, he will see justice done to them, and done speedily. But when the Son of Man comes, will he find any faith on earth?'

Persistence in Prayer

Luke stresses more than the other Gospel writers the importance of prayer in Jesus's own life. He depicts Jesus as praying at all the decisive moments of his life: as the Spirit descends on him at his baptism, before he chooses the Twelve. Then they catch him at prayer and ask him how to pray; he replies with the example of the Lord's Prayer. At the approach of his supreme test he prays confidently on the Mount of Olives and tells his disciples to pray in times of temptation. Finally at his Crucifixion he prays for the forgiveness of his executioners, and assures the penitent criminal that he will be this day in Paradise. We see him slipping away to pray in a lonely place in the early morning (4:42) or spending the whole night in prayer (6:12).

The present parable on persistence in prayer has all the Lukan features, such as lively dialogue and the chief actor asking himself what he should do next. Furthermore, like the advice on choosing a low place at table (14:8-9), the illustration seems to be based on the Wisdom Literature of the Old Testament: 'He [God] does not ignore the orphan's supplication nor the widow's as she pours out her complaint. Do the widow's tears not run down her cheeks as she accuses the man who is the cause of them?' (*Si* 35:14-15) - again it is a parable rather than an allegory, for in the Old Testament the responsive judge is God himself, not a corrupt human judge.

Jesus spoke the following parable to some people who prided themselves on being virtuous and despised everyone else: 'Two men went up to the Temple to pray, one a Pharisee, the other a tax collector. The Pharisee stood there and said this prayer to himself, "I thank you, God, that I am not grasping, unjust, adulterous like the rest of mankind, and particularly that I am not like this tax collector here. I fast twice a week; I pay tithes on all I get." The tax collector stood some distance away, not daring even to raise his eyes to heaven; but he beat his breast and said, "God, be merciful to me, a sinner." This man, I tell you, went home again at rights with God; the other did not. For everyone who exalts himself will be humbled, but the man who humbles himself will be exalted.'

The Pharisee and the Tax-Collector

This little scene gives us a forceful contrast about the attitude needed for prayer, the need simply to open ourselves to the Divine Mercy in humility and helplessness. Tax collectors were the most hated class of all. Morally they were despised and hated, since large firms bought the right to collect taxes and made their profits by ensuring that the money collected was well above what they had paid. Religiously they were despised because they worked for the unclean Romans. Yet here the tax-collector is the role-model - another instance of the role-reversal brought by Jesus: it is the rich who are poor and the poor who are rich.

Pharisees get a very bad press in the Gospels, partly because at the end of the first century, when the Gospels were being written, the Pharisees were the only group of the Jews remaining. So they stand for the Jewish opposition to Christianity. Was Jesus himself to opposed to them? They were the strictest group of the Jews, drawn from all strata of society, and helpful to one another. Because of their overriding regard for exact observance of the Law they were often at variance with Jesus, whose principle in legal observance was 'What I want is love, not sacrifice'. Yet in his discussions with them Jesus uses the same methods of arguing, quotation from scripture. The Pharisees took no part in the events which led to Jesus's death. Some think that the arguments between Jesus and the Pharisees were simply in-house discussions.

Jesus entered Jericho and was going through the town when a man whose name was Zacchaeus made his appearance; he was one of the senior tax collectors and a wealthy man. He was anxious to see what kind of man Jesus was, but he was too short and could not see him for the crowd; so he ran ahead and climbed a sycamore tree to catch a glimpse of Jesus who was to pass that way. When Jesus reached the spot he looked up and spoke to him: 'Zacchaeus, come down. Hurry, because I must stay at your house today.' And he hurried down and welcomed him joyfully. They all complained when they saw what was happening. 'He has gone to stay at a sinner's house' they said. But Zacchaeus stood his ground and said to the Lord, 'Look, sir, I am going to give half my property to the poor, and if I have cheated anybody I will pay him back four times the amount.' And Jesus said to him, 'Today salvation has come to this house, because this man too is a son of Abraham; for the Son of Man has come to seek out and save what was lost.'

Zacchaeus

This prosperous little man was not going to get any help from the Jericho crowd to help him catch sight of Jesus! The unpopularity of tax-collectors was in his case fully deserved; he had done very well out of the business, thank you! It just happened that he was too short to get a glimpse of Jesus. But he was resourceful enough to climb up a tree; you don't get rich without initiative. No sign that he had any religious motive; he just wanted to see what sort of guy this was who attracted such a crowd. Imagine, then, his delight when Jesus took the initiative and invited himself to dinner! It must have left him open-mouthed and full of joy that he should be picked out. Changed in a moment, he threw away all his old habits of mind to join this charismatic personality.

This is typical of Jesus with sinners. His opponents complained that he associated with the unclean and caroused with them, 'a glutton and a drunkard'. He didn't demand a promise of reform or good conduct; he just knew they needed him and he could help them make their lives different. So he went out to them. No pressure, just joy. It must have been impossible not to respond to the goodness of Jesus, impossible not to join him and follow his ways, whatever the cost. Such is the mercy of God.

Some Sadducees - those who say that there is no resurrection - approached Jesus and they put this question to him, 'Master, we have it from Moses in writing, that if a man's married brother dies childless, the man must marry the widow to raise up children for his brother. Well, then, there were seven brothers. The first, having married a wife, died childless. The second and then the third married the widow. And the same with all seven, they died leaving no children. Finally the woman herself died. Now, at the resurrection, to which of them will she be wife since she had been married to all seven?'

Jesus replied, 'The children of this world take wives and husbands, but those who are judged worthy of a place in the other world and in the resurrection from the dead do not marry because they can no longer die, for they are the same as the angels, and being children of the resurrection they are sons of God. And Moses himself implies that the dead rise again, in the passage about the bush where he calls the Lord the God of Abraham, the God of Isaac and the God of Jacob. Now he is God, not of the dead, but of the living; for to him all men are in fact alive.'

A Riddle of the Sadducees

This is the only full-blown appearance of the Sadducees in the Gospel, in a group of four confrontations between Jesus and different parties of the Jews, the elders, the Pharisees and Herodians, the Sadducees and the scribes. The Sadducees did not believe in any life after death, so here they are trying to make fun of the very idea of life after death. According to the Jewish Law, if I marry and die without begetting an heir, my nearest male relative must marry my widow and raise up children in my name, to continue my line. If this happens repeatedly (and seven, the perfect number, stands also for infinity), who is the husband in the after-life? Jesus cuts through the riddle, or rather goes behind it to the true understanding of scripture. In every case where a scriptural text is thrown at Jesus he replies at a deeper level of understanding. Here he returns to that fundamental revelation at the Burning Bush, 'I *am* the God of Abraham, Isaac and Jacob', protecting the family of Abraham from generation to generation and into the future. But things are different in the after-life. There is no marrying, no begetting of children. Nor is there any need for it, since in heaven there is no death and only perfect love. All is centred on God, the glory and mercy of God.

When some were talking about the Temple, remarking how it was adorned with fine stonework and votive offerings, Jesus said, 'All these things you are staring at now - the time will come when not a single stone will be left on another: everything will be destroyed.' And they put to him this question: 'Master,' they said 'when will this happen, then, and what sign will there be that this is about to take place?'

'Take care not to be deceived,' he said 'because many will come using my name and saying, "I am he" and, "The time is near at hand." Refuse to join them. And when you hear of wars and revolutions, do not be frightened, for this is something that must happen but the end is not so soon.' Then he said to them, 'Nation will fight against nation, and kingdom against kingdom. There will be great earthquakes and plagues and famines here and there; there will be fearful sights and great signs from heaven.

'But before all this happens, men will seize you and persecute you; they will hand you over to the synagogues and to imprisonment, and bring you before kings and governors because of my name - and that will be your opportunity to bear witness. Keep this carefully in mind: you are not to prepare your defence, because I myself shall give you an eloquence and a wisdom that none of your opponents will be able to resist or contradict. You will be betrayed even by parents and brothers, relations and friends; and some of you will be put to death. You will be hated by all men on account of my name, but not a hair of your head will be lost. Your endurance will win you your lives.'

Perseverance

We are beginning to approach the end of the liturgical year, and this passage sees Jesus looking beyond his death and Resurrection to the life of the Church. It is clear that Luke is writing after the Sack of Jerusalem and its Temple by the Romans in AD70. He speaks of not a stone left upon a stone, and indeed even today one can see the huge stones of the Temple wall thrown down by the Romans and still lying at its base. For Luke this is the symbol of the troubles which the disciples of Jesus will have to face up to: 'this will be your chance to bear witness to them... by your perseverance you will win your lives/souls.' The background to this must be the increasing persecutions undergone by Christians as they witnessed to their faith in the face of the Roman Empire, which called on them to worship the Emperor alone.

Indeed persecution has been a feature of Christianity throughout its existence, especially in the early centuries and again in the world of today. Low-level persecution comes to all of us who stand up to mockery and contempt for affirming our belief and Christian moral principles, but high-level persecution has been especially common in recent centuries producing martyrs in Uganda, Vietnam and Korea and in recent decades in the totalitarian states of Europe and the Far East, and in other countries such as Nigeria and Pakistan. There is plenty of room to thank God for the courage and perseverance of recent witnesses.

The people stayed there before the cross watching Jesus. As for the leaders, they jeered at him. 'He saved others,' they said 'let him save himself if he is the Christ of God, the Chosen One.' The soldiers mocked him too, and when they approached to offer him vinegar they said, 'If you are the king of the Jews, save yourself.' Above him there was an inscription: 'This is the King of the Jews.'

One of the criminals hanging there abused him. 'Are you not the Christ?' he said. 'Save yourself and us as well.' But the other spoke up and rebuked him. 'Have you no fear of God at all?' he said. 'You got the same sentence as he did, but in our case we deserved it: we are paying for what we did. But this man has done nothing wrong. Jesus,' he said 'remember me when you come into your kingdom.' 'Indeed, I promise you,' he replied 'today you will be with me in paradise.'

Christ's Kingship

The Crucifixion scene brings to a climax the work of the King of Mercy. Christ's Kingship is different from any other kingship, since it depends on love and loyalty rather than law. It is a response in love to his loving gifts. He earns his kingship by the salvation he offers us. He ends his life by saying, 'Father, into your hands I commit my spirit'; we know perfectly well that the Father will respond by raising him from the dead and sending his Spirit upon us.

Jesus's ministry in Jerusalem began with his weeping over the failure of the city to respond to his message. It ends with his telling the women of Jerusalem to mourn for themselves rather than for him. But then Jesus presides over a scene of general repentance and conversion, as God's mercy comes to fruition in the Crucifixion. He forgives his executioners; one of the criminals crucified with him confesses his guilt, and asks and receives assurance of his pardon. Finally the soldiers mock him with an irony which the reader perceives: they mock him for his inability to save himself, when we know that he saves not only himself but the whole world. So at his death the centurion 'gives glory to God' - how much did he understand, and what did he mean by this declaration? We Christians can see that he was right, though perhaps not understanding the import of his words. Finally the onlookers depart in repentance, marking the conversion of Jerusalem, which the stubborn city had till then refused.